Number 5

THOSE S.O.B.'S AT TARRYALL

●

And Other Tales

Of The Rockies

BY FRED HUSTON

Nortex
Press

Copyright 1974 by Fred Huston

Printed In The United States Of America
By Nortex Press
Quanah, Wichita Falls, Texas

Library of Congress Catalogue Card No. 74-79252
ISBN 0-89015-061-3

To Louise

whose insight and enthusiasm

(along with some nagging)

made this book,

and to a couple of pretty good kids,

Philip and Jeff.

Preface

The people you will meet, however briefly, in these pages are not those you find storied in legend, song and on television. There are no Billy the Kid types whispering "Quien es?" to a Pat Garrett in the dark of the night, no Wyatt Earps striding purposefully down the broad dirt street, ready for a shoot out with the local toughs. They are, I hope, different; people you haven't met before.

They range, in time, from Uncle Dick Wootton who first came to the Rockies in 1837 and stayed to become a legend to Sam Strong, a millionaire miner with a love for the ladies, the bottle and the wheel of chance who met his untimely end at the hands of a little known, readily forgotten bad man named Crumley. The stops in between cover a lot of people who left their mark, however unknowingly, on the pages of the west; those men from Wisconsin who are remembered as S.O.B.'s; Jim and John Reynolds who tried to cloak their larcenous instincts in the guise of fighting for a cause; Bob Ford, a murderer and Ford's killer, Ed Kelly, neither of whom were particularly missed by the rest of the world; Ed Frodsham, a pioneer and an innovator in organized banditry; a hapless sheriff caught in the middle of what could have been an even bloodier strike and finally, the story of a judge who didn't bother, for the best of reasons, to adjourn a term of court.

For the serious historian the book will offer little, unless he views history with tongue in cheek rather than as the be-all and end-all of scholarly attainment. The stories will, hopefully, entertain as they shed light on some of the lesser known inhabitants of early day Colorado. What may seem as character assassination is not intended as such; most of the facts presented herein have been gleaned from contemporary newspaper accounts (which were rougher than I could ever be, since in those days they called a spade a spade and a crook a crook) of the events; reminiscences of those who were contemporaries of the always colorful but sometimes inept characters offered here and in some cases conversations with those who either were witnesses or are closely associated with the places where the events occurred.

For gracious assistance in research material and pictures no amount of thanks could convey my gratitude to Mrs. Alys Freeze and Mr. James H. Davis of the Denver Public Library, Mrs. Alice Sharp of the State Historical Society of Colorado and Miss Brenda Hawley of the Penrose Public Library, Colorado Springs. And a special thanks to Cotton and Joan Gordon of the Tarryall River Ranch for introducing me to the spectacular land where those S.O.B.'s found their gold. I hope that none of them feel I have taken too many liberties with the facts in an attempt to make this book as much fun to read as it was to write.

TABLE OF CONTENTS

1. Those S.O.B.'s At Tarryall 1

2. Shoot Out In Newport Saloon 13

3. Lynch Law Comes To Leadville 23

4. Old Dick Wooten, He Had A Way With A Dollar 35

5. The Coward Killer Meets His End 49

6. The Texans Are Coming 62

7. General Tarsney's War 75

8. The Court That Never Adjourned 92

1 Those S.O.B.'s At Tarryall

It's bad enough to go down in history as an S.O.B., but even worse when your good name is damned by a combination horse thief and stage robber who attempted to cloak his thievery under the guise of being a Confederate raider. But such was the case for fourteen Wisconsin men who made their strike along the banks of one of Colorado's then unnamed creeks in the summer of 1859.

The S.O.B.'s weren't the first to enter the South Park to seek their fortunes. The original prospectors arrived in the early days of 1856, hoping to find gold of their own after having been unsuccessful in both Gregory Gulch and Central City. Working the banks of the Bayou Salado, William Slaughter, J.D. Kennedy and Dr. J.L. Shank found their color, but before they could determine its value they were set upon by some unfriendly Utes with a highly developed sense of property rights. Kennedy and Shank were killed in the attack which so discouraged Slaughter that he took his hair and went back to Central City to tell his fellows of the massacre.

The Utes had some justice on their side. For centuries they had roamed the valley of the South Platte and all of its tributaries including what would one day be called Tarryall Creek. To them it was not only a bit of home but a good place to hide from raiding Kiowa and Comanche warriors who were in the habit of crossing the plains to steal Ute horses. The Utes quite naturally had strong feelings about the occasional groups of crazy white men who came along and dug a bunch of useless holes in the ground. For a while after the killing of Shanks and Kennedy it was an unwary prospector who wandered into South Park alone.

The miners were incensed that the Indians could commit such an atrocity and promptly set about to organize a punitive expedition so that the savages might be properly chastised. The posse was barely off the ground when Slaughter admitted that although color had been found, it was hardly worth the effort it would take to get it out. The war-like miners promptly returned to the bar and had another;

leaving the Utes to breathe in peace a while longer.

Three years passed before another group of prospectors got discouraged enough to have a try at the new ground along the South Platte. These men, when they left their homes in Wisconsin, were probably neither more nor less S.O.B.'s than any other group picked at random throughout the eastern states. They had first tried the diggings around Cherry Creek but soon found that everything good was taken. The old hands watched their fumbling attempts and decided that this was just another bunch of hard luck johnny-come-latelies who would have to tough it out or head for home, richer in experience but poorer in pocket than when they left their homes.

As they wandered through the frozen mountains of Colorado, they certainly looked like the original hard luck bunch. They were hungry, quite tired, and more than a little discouraged. But like all of their predecessors, this tiny group acted as though their personal bonanza was just over the next ridge, somewhere along the next creek bed or dry wash.

In July the fourteen Badger state natives, W.J. Holman, E. Hamilton, W.J. Curtice, M.N.H. Spillard, Tom Cassady, A.D. Barnes, Bill Mitchum, Bill Horsemen, John Williams, James Merrill, C. Dale, T. Jenkins, John Aldrich and C. Chambers set out from Gregory Gulch for their date, if not with destiny, then at least with a slanderous appendage to their names that would last these hundred and thirteen years.

Leaving the Gulch they crossed over the Snowy Range near the head of Chicago Creek and passed through Buffalo Park. On the 19th of July they finally reached the Bayou Salado and pitched their tents, having dug in the gravel of all the stream beds along the way, finding a little color from time to time, but not enough to make them end their search. As they wandered across the valley, they found the cabins of the ill fated Slaughter party. But since fourteen armed men are more formidable than three, the original inhabitants let this party alone.

Although about as low as any men could be, the signs of human habitation had caused them to stop and begin a systematic search of the creek that was to become the Tarryall, and its tributaries, most of which were dry washes during the summer. Finding a likely looking gravel bar they sank a shaft and began the laborious task of raising the mud and silt to the top, then washing it and hoping against hope that there would be some nice heavy gold that would sink to the bottom of the sluice box and at least pay them wages for their efforts.

Their first two loads told them that they had finally hit it. Maybe not rich, but there was good color in the bottom of the rocker. After making their way across half of Colorado they had found gold, as one member of the party put it, in nuggets the size of watermelon seeds worth from a quarter to a dollar and a half apiece. And the nuggets weren't just an occasional thing, they appeared in abundance with each load that was washed.

Finding some logs to sit on, they organized a miner's meeting, the first thing that happened after any discovery, no matter how small. Among them they made arrangements to "tarry all" at this spot, and thus, however inadvertently named a town, a beautiful creek, the spectacularly beautiful mountains in the area and a mining district. Little did they know that Tarryall would soon be changed to Graball and that years later the name Tarryall would still be associated with S.O.B.'s.

They took full advantage of being there first, as had all the other early arrivals at the other Colorado strikes. Feeling that they were truly pioneers in the South Park, they set out to stake their claims. They weren't interested in the so-called hard rock variety, which by custom was three hundred feet wide and fifteen hundred feet long, but rather in placer claims, a full hundred and sixty acres.

Custom did not state the exact shape the claim should be, nor did it specify how it should conform the landscape, therefore, the original fourteen decided that they would make their own determination of shape and conformity. They all staked their placers, wedge shaped and of sufficient length to run from the middle of the creek to the ridge line, dooming any latecomers to hunt for their own dry washes and creek beds. As one of the men put it,

"Let them get wrinkles in their bellies like we did. If they want gold, let them find their own."

This probably wasn't an original sentiment confined to the Tarryall men. The impression is that they had heard it before, from Central City and Cherry Creek. But this spokesman surely was the first true S.O.B. at Tarryall.

E.N. Byers, the energetic editor of the *Rocky Mountain News* soon got wind of the strike and trumpeted the find in his boldest type. Early in August he commented on the steady stream of men on horseback, afoot, and in homemade carts leaving Denver for the new mines. It must not have been quite the mass exodus that Byers reported, since there were only about a hundred and fifty men in the camp that first winter.

The late arrivals were in poor shape both financially and physically. This was the last stampede of the season and all of the argonauts were low on funds needed to buy the necessities of life like flour and whiskey, mostly the latter. There was some development work to be had in Tarryall but not enough to tide a man over through the brutal months of winter.

The founding prospectors turned out to be philanthropists of a sort. They allotted a pit in the richest part of the district as a sort of savings bank for those who were down on their luck. Whenever a man needed a few dollars to help him over the rough spots, he went to the pit, known as Whiskey Hole, dug out whatever he needed and was able to keep himself in beans and booze. This act of charity on the part of the city fathers is somewhat tarnished when it is discovered that the owner of the pit was no longer in camp, having gone back east for the winter.

Spring of 1860 brought an influx of those who sought more or less instant wealth. They found the situation in regard to claims was still what it had been the year before. Not wishing to associate with those S.O.B.'s and convinced that the good claims on that side of the creek were gone, the newcomers went across the creek and started a town of their own, naming it Hamilton for one of the lesser S.O.B.'s. Still others went on up the Platte to found yet another town.

"In this camp," proclaimed Jim Reynolds, the erstwhile civic leader, thief and all around tough guy, "there'll be fairplay, not like those S.O.B.'s at Tarryall." Thus Reynolds named one camp and doomed the residents of another to an unflattering sobriquet that would be remembered long after their Christian names were forgotten.

Fairplay grew and remains a town to this day and the town across the creek, Hamilton, soon became a veritable metropolis on the mountain side, boasting such niceties of civilization as a wholesale provision house, a drug store, six groceries, a pair of physicians, a lawyer, a hotel, three boarding houses and a justice of the peace, (probably so that the lawyer would have someplace to try his cases.) Judging from this list Hamilton was a glowing light of morality in the annals of boom towns, since no saloons are listed. It must have been necessary to go across to Tarryall if you wanted to sin.

This might actually have been the case. Young Irving Howbert, who was to become one of the Cripple Creek millionaires and whose father was a Methodist minister reported that his father raised the money in Hamilton to build a church among those of his religious persuasion in less than a week.

By the summer of 1860 there were more than five thousand people in the Hamilton-Tarryall diggings, enough to prompt the city leaders to petition the government for a post office even though the town was not incorporated. They got not only mail service but three times a week stage service as well. Byers came to town and became the editor-publisher-printer of something called the "Miner's Record" but it lasted little more than a year. No one, it seems, was inclined to advertise their wares to such a limited audience.

Aside from the slanderous cognomen applied to the founders, Tarryall had several other claims to fame. It was the hometown of a private mint, it had what was easily the most inaccessible cemetery in the northern hemisphere and hardly anyone ever died there, with or without their boots on.

Tarryall served for a brief time as county seat of Park county although the town was never legally a town. Every time they tried to have an election of city officials so that they could qualify for incorporation, so many of the S.O.B.'s filed for mayor that no one could ever come up with anything like a clear cut majority. The mint, pride of the miners, was established in 1861 by John Parsons who manufactured gold coins in two fifty and five dollar denominations. The coins had a stamp mill on the face while the back was left blank. Mr. Parsons apparently found that Hamilton and Tarryall were not of sufficient size to support such an enterprise so he folded after a short while and went elsewhere.

Aside from the Utes, who became much more peaceful as soon as they were outnumbered, the camp was troubled very little. Only two outlaw gangs attempted to prey on the camp and they were both given short shrift. One bunch, the Espinosa gang, made a sad tactical mistake when they attempted to relieve the camp's top marksman, Tom Tobin, of the profits of his spring cleanup. Tobin cut down on the Espinosas with his rifle and buried two of the Espinosa brothers where they fell.

The Reynolds (the same one of Fairplay and S.O.B. fame) were run to ground near Tarryall, bringing to an end their somewhat abortive attempt to bring Colorado and all of its banks under the banner of the Confederacy. They, too, were buried where they fell to avoid the lengthy trip to the cemetery.

For reasons known only to the inhabitants of the camp, the cemetery was established nearly eleven miles from town on the top of a nearly vertical ridge. It has been said by some that those who planned to do in an enemy in or around Tarryall and Hamilton thought long and hard about the difficulty of burying his victim, then would give up the idea, deciding to wait until he could catch his victim in some town where the burial could be accomplished more easily.

The only killing on record in the camp occurred when the district was on the decline. It occurred in the 1890's, more than thirty years after the discovery of gold. A man described as a gentleman gambler named Craig shot at and might have killed P.O. Cox, a decidedly ungentlemanly saloon keeper.

Cox, according to those who knew him best, was an overbearing oaf who really needed to be killed. His major claim to fame was his ability to drink his own whiskey and still get up the next morning. This in itself was enough to condemn him in the eyes of his customers. Cox lost eighty dollars to Craig in a game of chance and was obviously unhappy about his losses. After the game he spent most of the next day drinking his own inventory and cleaning his rifle. Near nightfall he sneaked into Craig's favorite haunt, a dancehall, and hid behind the counter. The longer he waited the more he drank, peering blearily around the counter from time to time to see if Craig had appeared.

When Craig entered the dance hall, the place was filled with laughing women and cavorting miners. By this time, Cox was beyond the point where he could or would worry about innocent bystanders so he rose from his hiding place and let fly at Craig. The miners, who had been around a lot of tough camps, knew just what to do when the shooting started. They dove for cover, pulled their own guns and started blazing away; some at the ceiling, some at the floor, some at Cox and some in all directions just to hear the noise.

Apparently most of the miners, along with Craig, were trying to hit Cox. Feeling outnumbered and unloved, Cox dashed from his hiding place, only to fall dead on the porch. Craig, ever the gentleman, tried to borrow a horse so that he could ride over to Fairplay and surrender to the sheriff. The horseowners in the crowd, no matter their personal feeling for Craig, declined to lend him a horse, since they weren't sure that he would really go to Fairplay and even if he did, they weren't sure when or how they could get the horse home.

Aside from this small show of faithlessness, they all assured Craig that he was blameless in the death of Cox. With nearly everyone in town except the schoolteacher and the preacher shooting no one could be sure who killed Cox. Craig was the true Victorian hero, though, insisting that he give himself up since Cox might have lived, despite drinking his own whiskey, if Craig hadn't won all that money from him.

The sheriff rode into Tarryall the next morning, having heard of the ruckus. He arrested Craig, rented a horse for him and hauled him back to Fairplay to stand trial. The jury felt that Craig might have fired the fatal shot, so they sentenced him to two years in Canyon City. No more was heard of the gentleman gambler of the Tarryall diggings.

Tarryall nearly died in the early seventies but was revived by more efficient corporate mining operations, organized to find and recover the deposits of gold and silver that individual miners were unable to bring to the surface. But by the end of the century, the town was down to two hundred people, and by 1933, only four residents remained. Now there are none. The site is even hard to find and once found, even harder to recognize as the location of two once booming communities. There aren't even the remains of the wholesale provision house or the Methodist Church.

The cemetery is still there provided you have the strength to make the climb although most of the markers have fallen victim to the ravages of time. One old timer insists that he can still walk to the Whiskey Hole but he won't do it and is reluctant to tell anyone else how to go about it. Spruce, pine and aspens have grown through the grass that now covers the old tailings. Not even the headworks of the old mines are anywhere in evidence any more.

The original S.O.B.'s left few marks on the pages of history. Most of them made a little money, sold out and left the country. But no matter what their accomplishments might have been in later life, they are still remembered in the books and stories of the gold strikes as "those S.O.B.'s at Tarryall."

WILLIAM SLAUGHTER saved his hair and his life after raiding Utes killed his two partners on the first prospecting trip into the Tarryall region. Photo—Colorado Historical Society.

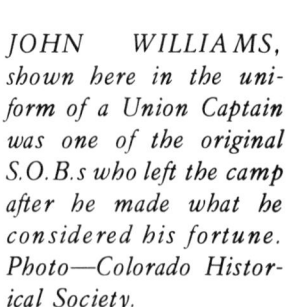

JOHN WILLIAMS, shown here in the uniform of a Union Captain was one of the original S.O.B.s who left the camp after he made what he considered his fortune. Photo—Colorado Historical Society.

LONG ABANDONED log storage building near the site of Tarryall.

THE VALLEY of the Tarryall, where nuggets the size of watermelon seeds could be forced from the ground.

ROUNDHOUSE AT Como, Colorado on the old Denver, South Park and Pacific near the towns of Tarryall and Hamilton.

LONG ABANDONED depot at Como.

REMAINS OF prospectors' cabin in Tarryall mountains of Central Colorado.

MINER'S CABIN in the hills between Fairplay and Tarryall in the 1860's. Photo—Colorado Historical Society.

THE ROAD TO Tarryall leads through what is left of the more or less modern day town of the same name. The schoolhouse is now deserted.

THE ICE COMES early to Tarryall Creek above the eight thousand foot level.

 ## Shoot Out In The Newport Saloon

One might say that Grant Crumley's Newport Saloon in Cripple Creek was going full blast in the early morning hours of August 23, 1901. Actually, the blast came from Grant's equalizer, .a sawed off ten gauge shotgun he was using at the moment to remove parts of Sam Strong's head, thereby settling an argument that had waxed and waned for several weeks. It turned out to be the most sensational killing in the Cripple district until Harry Orchard dispatched several innocent bystanders when he dynamited the Independence Depot more than a year later.

Sam Strong could hardly have been called a civic leader, although he was one of the more successful prospectors who had entered the golden bowl in 1891 to seek his fortune. A lumber hauler and roughneck in Colorado Springs, he had come across the mountains almost the complete tenderfoot, but with good sense to follow in the footsteps of the man who was to become Cripple's richest citizen, Winfield Scott Stratton, an unemployed carpenter.

Strong, along with two Springs' municipal employees, Burns and Doyle, a grocer named Dowdy and one McKinnie, a carpenter's helper had settled on the slopes of Battle Mountain, just down hill from Stratton's fabulously wealthy Independence. All of them struck it rich.

From all reports it was a jolly group along the side of the mountain. All were bachelors, all were suddenly coming into unimagined wealth. They spent their off hours having a sociable nap or two, either in their cabins or in the numerous saloons in Victor and Cripple, usually winding up an evening's entertainment in one of the houses that lined both sides of Cripple's Myers Avenue. But whatever their pleasure, all could afford it.

After finding his gold, Sam had set to work to develop the claim as rapidly as one man with no capital could manage it. When two Colorado Springs financiers offered Sam sixty thousand for an option on the mine, the rowdy teamster was well on his way to becoming a millionaire. Although he might have lived longer (if not happier) had he stayed on the lumber wagon. Sam took his money and went into the investment and grubstake business and soon numbered among his properties not only the Strong mine but the well paying Free Cosinage, also on Battle Mountain.

Sam first crossed paths with Grant Crumley during the strike of 1894 when Crumley along with an assorted group of toughs, many of them ex Denver policemen, were hired by the mine owners and formally deputized to help break the strike. As the deputies rode up the hill to Victor and Altman, the striker's stronghold, they were stunned by the sight of the Strong Mine's headworks rising majestically into the air propelled by a large charge of dynamite placed there by the strikers.

This was rougher than the deputies had bargained for, so they headed back down the hill, urged along the way by a loose flat car that had been loaded with explosives and headed down the track. With their deputy jobs gone, some went back to their previous employment (robbery and extortion) for the ubiquitous Soapy Smith in Denver while others hung around to see if they could make more money fleecing miners than they could mining for gold. Crumley was among those who stayed, proving he was no bigot by joining the forces of "Generals" Junius Johnson and Jack Smith, leaders of the criminal faction of the striking miners. But all good things must end and soon the strike was over, forcing Grant to look for some other form of employment.

With his brothers, Sherman and Newt, who, some said, had ridden with the Daltons, Grant set up shop in Victor as a steerer for the Crumley gang. The sons of an Alabama minister, the brothers were not particularly adept at the bandit business, certainly not as much so as the Daltons, although it was a living. The end came when Grant, working as a dealer in a saloon, noticed three strangers who seemed to have more than their fair share of money.

Grant contacted his brothers who discovered that the tourists were leaving on the midnight train. With Sherman serving as lookout, three members of the gang, Bob Taylor, Kid Wallace and O.C. Wilder stopped the train and relieved the travelers of their money and jewelry.

The money was divided and the jewelry sent to Denver so that Soapy Smith could fence it. But as thieves will, the gang fell out, with one of the members who had been left out of the robbery (and the split) blowing the whistle on the others. The result was that Wilder, Taylor and Wallace were given lodging in the state hotel at Canyon City. Sherman, who had been along on the job but hadn't been seen by the victims, was exonerated. But it seemed the good old days of being a highwayman were over, so the three brothers went into the saloon and high grading business, which put them in the way of Sam Strong who seems to have spent more than a normal amount of time in such places of recreation.

Not that Sam was vice ridden. He smoked, of course, but that wasn't a vice in those dim days before the Reader's Digest, just a habit. He probably had an occasional chew during the day. But what he really did enjoy, although he did it badly, was gambling. And like so many poor players, he hated to lose. He rather enjoyed the bottle, usually more than was good for his health and he liked the ladies. Not just one lady at a time, but several ladies. And they obviously enjoyed either his company or his money. Actually, it got to the point where the more money Sam had in his pocket, the more sex appeal he seemed to have. It finally got to the point where he figured the best way out of his dilemma was marriage.

In 1900 Sam was thirty eight and still the completely unpolished millionaire, but he felt he needed a wife. He chose nineteen year old Regina Neville of Altman. The young lady might have been deluded into thinking that Sam was quite a catch, but she was soon disabused of this notion.

No sooner had the service ended than Sam was served with a summons. It seemed that one of the young Cripple Creek ladies of his acquaintance needed a quarter of a million dollars to soothe her injured feelings. Sam, she said, had been promising to marry her since '92 or '93 and she felt he had been unfair when he took up with Miss Neville.

This suit was no sooner out of the way then a former paramour from Goldfield appeared and filed against Sam for the same amount. A half million lighter, Sam and Regina finally left for a honeymoon in Europe, to return the following year.

With his marriage seriously limiting his escapades with women, Sam started taking his drinking and gambling more seriously on his return to the goldfields. Money was no problem since he still had better than three quarters of a million dollars to spend, with more coming in every day. After a try at Colorado Springs society, which gave Sam, ever the roughneck, a cold shoulder, the couple settled in

Cripple Creek.

On August 22, 1901, with Regina off to Denver on a shopping spree, Sam was left at loose ends. In company with his father-in-law John Neville, who served as chaperone and his secretary, Clarence Fitch as a companion, Sam set out to hit the high spots in the golden city, winding up just before dawn in Crumley's saloon in the Mining Exchange building.

Sam and Grant had had harsh words only a few weeks earlier when Strong, having dropped twenty five hundred dollars on a Crumley table paid the debt with a check. Before Crumley could get to the bank the next morning, Strong had payment stopped, claiming the that Grant was running a crooked table. With the Crumley reputation it might have been true, but since he hadn't forced Sam to play, Crumley felt that he was being ill used. The matter was finally settled to the satisfaction of no one with Strong paying Crumley two hundred dollars.

Crumley wasn't too pleased to see the Strong party stagger into the Newport, stop for a drink and then head for the roulette wheel. Both Neville and Fitch were trying to get Strong to call it a night and head for home, but the miner would have none of it and shortly found himself about a hundred and fifty dollars ahead. When Crumley passed the table, Sam, ever the diplomat, called out,

"Well, Grant, I see you have finally got an honest game."

Crumley, seeing that the other two men were trying to get Strong back on the street, let the remark pass. But thinking it over, he had a change of heart. Perhaps if Strong stayed he could get even with him again. When Sam left for the men's room, Grant came over and started to remonstrate with the two men.

"Leave the people alone in my house," he said. "I won't have you coming in here and trying to get people to leave."

He was still at it when Strong returned from a brief visit to the restroom. He grabbed Crumley and with something of a flair for overstatement yelled,

"Here now, this is my daddy and I won't have you pushing him around."

"Like hell he's your daddy," Crumley replied, trying to shake Strong off. No mention is made of how Neville felt about being credited with Strong's paternity.

Fitch intervened, assuring Crumley that Neville was Sam's father-in-law, if not his daddy, whereupon Crumley apologized and suggested that they all have a drink on the house.

Shaking hands, they trooped to the bar, with the already liquor logged Sam in the lead, while Fitch and Neville tried to get him out of the place and hopefully home in bed.

As Sam poured himself a drink Crumley put his hands in his pockets and leaned against the back bar. Something about the pose enraged Sam, for he reached into his pocket, pulled a pistol and shouted,

"Get your hands out where I can see him, Crumley. Bring them out empty or I'll kill you where you stand."

Faced with the pistol, Crumley promptly complied, while Fitch and a bystander named Prentice grabbed Strong and tried to wrestle the pistol away from him. Some witnesses said he returned the gun to his pocket, others said it was pointing at the floor and still others that it was behind his back. Whatever the position of the gun, Crumley had had enough Sam Strong for one night. Ducking behind a screen that separated the cigar counter from the bar he appeared to be trying to get away from Strong and the pistol.

Fitch, with Strong still in his grasp, started for the door. As they passed the cigar counter (again, according to some, others say they were still in front of the bar) Grant Crumley raised up with a shot gun and let fly, the number four shot tearing a chunk out of Strong's skull just above the right eye. It was just as well, according to the medical report, that Grant had given up the road agent business. He fired from a distance of under two feet and still missed his victim with most of the shot. Fitch, who had been justifiably alarmed when Crumley appeared with the shotgun had let go of his charge and hit the floor just before the shot.

As Strong fell, Neville took off for the drugstore in search of a doctor. Those who stayed, and they were few, since most of the patrons found that a quick trip to the back door was the safest route to a speedy exit, helped move Strong to his mother-in-law's house, then went out to send for his wife.

Sam lived about three hours, never regaining consciousness. Grant surrendered to the local law and was lodged in the VIP suite of the new city jail to await the convening of a coroner's jury. After being lodged in jail, Grant was quoted as saying he hadn't been aware that he had so many friends. Or perhaps that there were so many people that couldn't stand Sam Strong.

Regina Strong was notified in Denver that an accident had befallen her husband, but not that he was breathing his last. She caught the first train south and was advised when she reached Colorado Springs that Sam had died.

The coroner's inquest brought out several interesting facts, not the least of which was that most of the witnesses scattered at the sound of the shot. Nearly everyone who testified intimated that they had seen and heard everything up to and including the shot and some had even seen Sam start to fall, but after that they were rather vague. Only Clarence Fitch seems to have stayed for the whole event.

Fitch testified about the bad feelings between the two men; the harsh words that had passed about Strong's "daddy" and the handshake, but that following expressions of good will, the situation deteriorated and Sam wound up dead on the floor.

The body of the late Sam Strong was released to his widow for burial in Denver, while Crumley was bound over for the September term of court with bail set at fifty thousand dollars. The bail was promptly raised by brother Elks and assorted bartenders and gamblers that the newspaper euphemistically referred to as "storekeepers."

The trial was anticlimatic, with Crumley being promptly acquitted by a jury of his peers. The jurors assumed, with some degree of accuracy, that Grant was, for once, defending himself. Since Strong had drawn a gun and threatened his killer it made no difference, in the eyes of the jurors, where the gun happened to be pointing at the time Crumley unlimbered the shotgun.

Cripple had reached and passed its peak by the time of the shooting and soon thereafter it started on a slide to virtual oblivion, only to be partially revived in recent years by a steady influx of tourists. The town of Victor still stands, in a manner of speaking, but the others, Goldfield and Alma included, along with the headworks of the once rich mines have slowly rotted away and fallen victim to vandals who have stripped them for firewood and scrap metal.

Cripple made no more millionaires out of wandering teamsters and as the town slowly died, the Grant Crumleys moved on to lesser and lesser things until the boom towns of the west all shared pretty much a common grave with the Sam Strongs who had made them.

ALTHOUGH THE Methodists seem to have disappeared, the beer drinkers remain. Boarded up doors of church reflect the condition of most of the buildings in Cripple except those in tourist related businesses.

CRIPPLE HAS BECOME a rather lively ghost with summer subdivisions being staked off daily in the hills which once reverberated to the sounds of the whistle punk and the donkey engine. The town itself presents a forlorn appearance from the top of the mountains to the north of the onetime Golden City.

HARDLY A BUILDING in Victor, once the headquarters of the Crumley gang, have escaped the random vandalism that empty buildings seem to attract. Onetime Christian Science church is no exception.

THE VICTOR RECORD, once the voice of a booming little city, is now boarded and silent.

BATTLE MOUNTAIN was covered with millionaire making mines. This is reportedly the Strong Mine when in full production. Photo—Denver Public Library.

ROTTING HEADWORKS of once rich mining properties and the crumbling brick walls of once thriving towns dot the hills in the Golden Bowl that was the Cripple Creek district.

IN THE LATE nineties everyone lined the walk (just as they do today) to wave at and pose for the photographer. And little boys show off their favorite toy of the moment, in this case a sterrable sled. Photo—Denver Public Library.

SAM STRONG loses his hat and his head as Grant Crumley lets fly with the ten gauge bar shotgun. Photo—Denver Public Library.

 *Lynch Law Comes To Leadville*

Whatever else Ed Frodsham might have been, he was no small time operator when he decided to go into the real estate business in the booming camp of Leadville, Colorado. Nor was his exit any less spectacular. He had the dubious honor of becoming the first customer for the vigilantes of the town on a cold November night in 1879.

His companion dangling from the rafters of a partially completed building was a former employee of the Stick Up Division of what nowadays would be called Frodsham Industries. He was Charles, or Patrick Stewart, depending on who one asks. Both were there as a result of actions considered by the residents of the carbonate camp to be both illegal and downright brazen in character. Even a mining camp can stand only so much outrage and the Frodsham boys had passed that point.

Little is known of the early life of Leadville's criminal boss whose full, and totally unlikely, name was Edwin V. Frodsham. He first appears on the western scene at Deadwood, but there he had little chance to make a reputation, being a mere novice bad man tossed into a pond containing hundreds of the real item. He had, according to some of the people in Leadville, served a term for murder in Wyoming and had been accused of another, although he was never brought to trial for the second offense. He had learned from his troubles in Laramie; never again would he hold the gun or pull the trigger. In the future he would do the brain work and devote his time to more gainful pursuits, such as counting the ill gotten gains or his now burgeoning real estate business. Punks to carry a gun could, he reasoned, be hired.

Bitter experience had shown Frodsham that claim jumping in the mountains around Leadville was both an expensive and risky business. The mine owners had taken to hiring armed guards and at least two pitched battles had been fought over a couple of the more lucrative claims. The business of lot jumping in a town where the price of land might quadruple over a three day period seemed to be a much better deal. No one would be inclined to hire an army to protect a twenty five foot lot. Frodsham hired some gunslingers to be lot acquisition specialists leaving Frodhsam free to handle the sales, and the money, himself.

Lot jumping was a simple business. You merely occupied the property with a few gun toting toughs while the owner was away or, if he happened to be at home, you threw him out. Buildings, either totally or partially completed, were no problem. Since most of them were merely shacks, you tore them down and threw the lumber out in the street along with the previous owner's belongings.

The summer of 1879 saw hold ups and lot jumping reach a peak in Leadville. Robberies were so commonplace that few ventured away from the main streets after nine in the evening. Businessmen who were forced to work late were in the habit of hiring a policeman to escort them home. The common morning greeting around Leadville was,

"How many hold ups last night?"

Although a formally organized town in an organized county, Leadville, with its highly transient population, was an excellent field for one of Ed Frodsham's talents. The courts were crowded and the judges not noted for their zeal. The police had barely time to take the crime reports, let alone go running around the mountains chasing criminals and trying to bring them to justice, such as it was.

By the fall of '79 Frodsham, who apparently was arrested every day and released with the same frequency, had moved his attention to a rapidly developing section of the city known as Capitol Hill, along Lincoln Avenue and Pine Street. He had no need to develop subtlety in his dealings in lot piracy, as this example of confused titles and forcible takeovers indicates.

Three claimants to one lot lived together in a hastily thrown together shanty. Two of the residents, an ex-jailer named Michael Cooney and M.J. Redding decided they would dispossess the third, a man identified as Moore. The forcibly removed Moore, his bedding and gear, and told him that any claim he had on the property was null and void.

Moore was considerably miffed by this turn of events so he rounded up still another claimant, N.N. Robertson and returned to the shack. Cooney and Redding were out at the time, so their effects were removed, a log propped against the door to serve as a lock and the new owners went to bed.

About three in the morning they were awakened by a loud knock. The caller was asked what he wanted and he answered that he wished to discuss business. Robertson and Moore told the visitor, somewhat emphatically, that they discussed business only during normal hours so the caller would have to wait.

The nocturnal visitor tried to batter the door down with little success, and turning, he called to what must have been a good sized crowd of followers for help and started shooting into the shack. Witnesses reported that some sixty or seventy shots were fired before Robertson and Moore decided to move, leaving the house and lot to the new owner, Ed Frodsham. It was noted in the Chronicle the next day that,

"Unfortunately for the public taste, no one was killed."

Like most racketeers, Frodsham never knew when to quit, finally outraging the public to the extent that they put him under twenty four hour surveillance, feeling that they could expect no help from the law. The situation, as far as the law abiding citizens of Leadville were concerned, was becoming desperate. Frodsham's downfall was finally brought about by one of his employees when the tough young Stewart fouled up a hold up in company with either one or two other men, depending on who tells the story.

Not that Stewart was a particularly inept bandit, but after months of no opposition and no punishment, he became careless. On the night of November 15, 1879, Stewart and a man named Clifford, who was wanted for stage robbery in Texas, picked the wrong victim. It proved to be a fatal mistake for both the gunmen and Frodsham as well.

They didn't accidentally accost a gunman, but they ran afoul of a thoroughly frightened barber named Bockhaus, on his way home after an evening on the town. Bockhaus, whose first name seems to have escaped into history without leaving a trace, had little to lose in the way of money, but he had an aversion to being pistol whipped and slapped around. With those thoughts in mind, he had armed himself with a .22 pistol which he carried in his right hand as he walked home. Suddenly he was stopped by the command,

"Up with your hands!!!"

In later accounts Bockhaus admitted that he hadn't even thought of the gun until he started to raise his arms. As they came level he fired twice, according to some, three times according to others. This not only wounded but so unnerved the robbers that they ran off down the street. Bockhaus, not being cast in much of an heroic mold, ran the other way, straight into the arms of a policeman who had heard the shots and was on his way to see what it was all about. Stewart had run completely out of luck. He ran into another officer coming from the opposite direction who relieved him of his Colt which had two empty chambers.

Bockhaus' policeman didn't believe his story and escorted him to the scene where they met Stewart and the other officer. Since Stewart was sure that he would be free by morning, he readily admitted his part in the shooting, but said he hadn't seen his partner since they fled the scene. Stewart was slightly wounded and Bockhaus was sure that he had also hit Clifford, which was pretty good shooting for a frightened man with a little gun.

As the officers began to search the neighborhood, a man came to the door of his house and asked the police what they were looking for. They replied that they were looking for a wounded man, a hold up artist, that might be in the vicinity. The householder said that he didn't know anything about wounded people but if they happened to want a dead man, there was one on his back porch. Sure enough, there lay Clifford with a hole in his stomach. He had lived barely long enough to get out of the street.

Bockhaus immediately became the hero of the evening. Nearly a thousand people crowded through the morgue to see the body of one of Frodsham's feared henchmen, then headed for the nearest saloon to try and buy Bockhaus a drink. To make room for the morbidly curious, some five hundred left the bar and lined the streets to see Stewart escorted to jail from the doctor's office where he had been taken to have his wound treated. Bockhaus, it was said, didn't buy a drink with his own money for the next eight days.

The following Sunday they had a parade in Leadville, complete with a brass band. Bockhaus, the unassuming barber, was hoisted in a chair to the shoulders of the celebrants and carried triumphantly through town. That day, despite the adulation of the crowd, Bockhaus was nervous. Threats had been made against his life by persons completely capable of carrying them out; threats that apparently never had a chance to come to pass.

As the parade neared Chestnut Street, some of the marchers decided that since Bockhaus had done away with one robber, it might be well if they disposed of the other. Suddenly the cry was raised,

"To the jail . . . Let's hang that other SOB."

County officials, warned by the growing outcry, moved Stewart to the County Jail, a more substantial structure, where they were able to drive the mob away before Stewart was harmed. But his reprieve was to be short, for while the riff raff had been parading some of the town's more substantial citizens were in a meeting, hastily called, laying plans to rid the town and the county not only of the hold up men, but of their leader, Ed Frodsham, as well.

It was decided that since Stewart was already in jail they would prevail on the sheriff to leave him there. Now the problem was to get Frodsham in the same jail for more than a few minutes so that they could make him the prime horrible example to the criminal element. The trouble was, up to that time he had never stayed in custody long enough for even a two or three man lynch mob to form.

Some of the more nervous underworld characters, the bunko steerers and con men saw the handwriting on the wall when the mob stormed the jail durng the parade and began to pack and quietly leave town for greener and less volatile pastures. But the tough element, the gun toters and the lot jumpers, along with their boss, Frodsham, refused to heed warnings that their time was growing short and that if they had any idea of leaving Lake Country alive, they had best be on their way.

The first chance to cut off the serpent at the head came on Tuesday, November 18th when Frodsham was arrested on the complaint of some citizen who wished to have his misappropriated lot returned to his custody. On the advice of his lawyer, who obviously had his finger on the pulse of the community, Frodsham settled out of court and the complaint was dropped.

But the press of business wouldn't let Frodsham rest. There were so many lots to be had and pigeons to be plucked that he couldn't take even a day away from his appointed rounds. On Wednesday, along with his henchmen, he went to a lot where a house was being built. They ran off the workmen, pulled down the house and offered the lot for sale. By now the town was all out of patience with the killer from Wyoming and insisted to the elected officials that he once again be arrested, this time for disturbing the peace. The sheriff, tired of arresting the same man over and over again, put it off as long as he could, then picked Ed up about midnight and placed him in jail again.

The cage of the new county jail was filled with lawbreakers of various degrees, including the now notorious Stewart who had been entertaining his cell mates with boasts about being the best in the hijacking business. He also told them of his future plans, which included shooting anyone he wished to rob first rather than running the risk of crossing another Bockhaus.

Frodsham was treated as a guest rather than a prisoner and placed on a cot in the jail corridor to await the arrival of his lawyer. Since he rarely spent more than a few hours in custody he was not considered much of an escape risk. But tonight was different. No sooner had Frodsham been jailed than small groups of men, three or four at a time, appeared on the streets, never in a bunch large enough to cause suspicion.

Undersheriff Watson left the jail to go home shortly before one the morning of November 19th. He noticed the men seemingly loafing around the corners and in front of the saloons but thought little of it until he left the brightly lit main street. He was immediately surrounded by masked men, pointing pistols at the startled lawman. After disarming him they told the undersheriff that they had no wish to harm him, a statement that dried at least a little of the perspiration that had formed on his forehead, but that they did require entrance to the jail, since they had some rather important business to attend to there. Watson told them that the jail was locked from the inside and that he had no keys.

"Fine," he was told, "then we'll take you to the jail, you tell the jailer to unlock the door. And just to make sure that he doesn't get any wild ideas, you can walk in front of us. Then if the jailer wants to shoot, you'll be the first to go."

Back to the jail went the undersheriff, while passersby along Harrison Avenue were being stopped and told that there were some touchy matters being attended to and that they had best wait until things were settled before they proceeded. Since the requests were made by men with ready guns, the people agreed they had no business that couldn't wait until later.

The jailer, hearing the familiar voice of Watson, opened the door and was promptly disarmed. One other jailer, perched on top of the cage, was ordered to throw down his guns. Frodsham, seeing the masked men, had joined the jailer on his lofty perch. It seems that like so many tough types, Frodsham had no stomach for mobs who were after his hide. As soon as the jail door had opened he had climbed to the top of the cage and begged for protection from the law he had flaunted all his life.

The guard had little interest in protecting Ed. He was, understandably, more interested in living until the end of his shift. Frodsham was removed from the top of the cage and bound. He begged to write a letter to his wife, but was told there was no time for letter writing that night. Carried to a building under construction (some say it was to be the courthouse), a rope was placed around his neck, then passed over a joist. Frodsham was raised, kicking and struggling, and probably strangling.

Back to the jail went the vigilantes, this time for the boastful young Stewart to put an end to a less than illustrious career. Stewart, in a sudden burst of filial piety, wanted to write his mother a letter. It appeared that impending hanging brought out a literary urge in even the most unlettered.

"Write her in the morning," one of his captors grunted as they tied and gagged him, then escorted him to the same joist that supported the lifeless body of his former employer. Up went the rope, then up went Stewart. A note, probably the most quoted in the west, was pinned to the bodies.

"Notice," it read, "to all lot thieves, bunko steerers, footpads, thieves and chronic bondsmen for the same and sympathizers with the above class of criminals: this is our commencement and this shall be your fates. We mean business and let this be your last warning. Vigilantes Committee. We are seven hundred strong."

The note probably didn't do nearly as much good as the bodies swaying in the light breeze of the frigid morning. It was reported in the local paper that despite threats on the lives of the committee members and particularly barber Bockhaus, some four hundred people left Leadville at the first light of day. So many left, in fact, that only Mrs. Frodsham and the Reverend Claggett made it to the funeral. Four men had to be drafted from a nearby saloon to carry the coffin to the cemetery.

It was noted however, that the saloons that had catered to the Frodsham mob were on a twenty-four hour day, filled to the brim with erstwhile toughs who were afraid to go out on the streets. So they whiled away their time writing anonymous notes to the vigilantes and waited for a chance to escape.

The inquest following the hangings was a sell out. People came from miles around to hear jurors W.F. Hogan, Dennis Findley, John

Parks, Henry W. Gaw, William C. Miller and Giles Fonda exonerate the law officers and condemn mob violence but return no indictments.

Frodsham's ghost played a brief return engagement in January, 1880 when George Bush and William Trimble bought a lot on Harrison Avenue. The lot was jumped by a man named Shoemaker, who tore down the shack and tossed the lumber into the street. His occupancy was short lived since Trimble and Bush took the matter to court. When Shoemaker produced a Frodsham title, his right to the lot was declared void.

The last of the lot jumpers appeared on the scene in the spring of 1880, matched against some rather unlikely opponents. The would be jumpers discovered that the land on which the Sisters of Charity had built St. Vincent's Hospital had some value. The Rio Grande Western planned to be build their depot just north of the land held by the sisters, thereby increasing its value considerably.

The first threats were the usual anonymous letters. (It seems that the criminal element in Leadville was much given to literary pursuits.) The ladies refused to be intimidated and went on about the healing business. Then, on April 10, they received a message that the hospital would be fired on at ten that night unless the premises were vacated.

Father Robinson and Sister Superior Mary Bridgett felt that things were going a little too far so they rounded up some armed parishoners and stationed them about the grounds. At eleven, two men slipped through the fence and were ordered to halt. The command was ignored until someone fired a pistol, then the intruders ran off. Another shot and one of the lot jumpers fell. His companion stopped to help him to his feet and both were arrested by officer Sweeney. The unwounded man was shown the most direct route out of town. The injured man was treated by the Sisters, then run out of town.

Leadville settled down, helped in the process by a man with a new and novel idea of how to succeed in real estate with a minimum investment; a thoroughly frightened barber with a gun, and a teenage hold up artist with more than his allotted share of over confidence. Three ingredients were combined to end the career of the real estate man and the gunman, make a hero of the barber and establish the law of Judge Lynch in the carbonate camp of Leadville.

HOWLAND SKETCH of the carbonate camp called Leadville. Photo—Colorado Historical Society.

RICH CARBONATE MINES in the Leadville mountains were first targets of claim jumpers. When owners hired armed guards, Frodsham turned his attention to the more easily acquired town lots. Photo—Denver Public Library.

HANGINGS DREW A good crowd in Leadville even when they were legal. This dual execution seems to have emptied the town. Photo—Denver Public Library.

LEADVILLE IN THE late 1870's was undergoing a considerable building boom. Clouded and in some cases non existent titles made lot jumping an easy and profitable enterprise. Photo—Colorado Historical Society.

PAST DAYS of glory are reflected in Leadville City Hall, an almost perfect example of Victorian municipal architecture.

LEADVILLE HAD AN abundance of places handy for those intent on lynching, including this now abandoned livery stable.

NO PHOTOGRAPHERS were on the scene when vigilantes took their victim to the nearest rafter, allowing artist's imagination to run wild. Painting—Denver Public Library.

VIEW OF Leadville, late 1870's. Photo—Colorado Historical Society.

4. Old Dick Wooten, He Had A Way With A Dollar

"Two bits," said the grizzled old mountain man as he stepped out on the porch of the big adobe near the summit of Raton Pass.

"What do you mean, two bits?" grumbled the rider, eyeing the chain stretched across what passed for a road in the Rockies. "I could jump that little chain and be on my way before you could get off the porch, old man."

"I suppose you could, but how far would you get?" the elderly man replied, lifting a fifty caliber carbine from its resting place behind a post on the porch.

The rider, although maybe a tenderfoot, immediately saw the wisdom in the old man's words and reached into his faded jeans and came up with the price. The chain was dropped and he went on his way.

Richens Lacy "Uncle Dick" Wootton added another quarter to his toll road income, the final money maker for this strange combination, a mountain man who made money and then, unlike most of his contemporaries, managed to keep it. Wootton, who had spent fifty-six of his seventy-seven years in the deserts and the mountains of the west, was a living anachronism.

Wootton was a native Virginian and considered a well educated man for his time, having had what would probably amount now to a sixth grade education. He made his first trip west in the spring of 1837 with the train operated by the firm of Bent and St. Vrain, which moved from Independence, Missouri to Bent's Fort on the Arkansas loaded to the bows with trade goods. According to Wootton's account there were a hundred and forty wagons in the train, served by two hundred men.

Probably all of the two hundred would have been more than ready to hang their new tenderfoot swamper after an unforgettable night on Little Cow Creek, just east of the Cimarron cut off on the old trail. Wootton was standing night guard, a job for which he had been eminently well suited in the more settled areas of eastern Kansas, But now, alone in the land of Pawnee, Cheyenne and occasional Kiowa he tended to take the job much more seriously. Just as the teamsters had gotten the stock quiet and settled down for the night, a shot split the cool night air.

Since every man slept with a rifle, the shot brought them scrambling from their blankets, armed and ready to do battle with the heathen. Under the wagons they rolled, eyes peeled for the first sight of the savages. When none appeared, lanterns were lit and a search was started for Wootton's target. Sure enough, there on the ground lay a dead mule. He didn't really look much like an Indian now, but in the dark shadows of the cottonwoods he had somehow had a more menacing appearance. Wootton's start on the plains could hardly have been considered an auspicious one.

When the train arrived at Bent's Fort Wootton was sent out with some of the firm's more experienced hands to trade for robes and furs with the Sioux and the Crow to the north. He must have been considered, after the escapade on Cow Creek, an expendable employee, for although Bent and St. Vrain had a virtual monopoly south of the Platte, due to their close association with the southern or Hair Rope Cheyenne, the country to the north was considered the sole preserve of the powerful American Fur Company. Wootton's group, undaunted by the threats of their competitors, traded all the way past Laramie to the Rawhide and came home, not only with robes but with their hair as well.

After learning the ropes, Wootton engaged for a couple of years as a free trapper, learning the mountains and the ways of the people. When the beaver trade began to wane he returned to the fort, serving as a contract hunter, and learning yet another trade, one which he would follow most of the rest of his life, that of wagon boss for the Bent-St. Vrain trains running from the fort to the Santa Fe-Taos area.

January of 1847 gave Uncle Dick his first chance at the hero business, without which none of the mountain men would have ever been remembered. He was resting at the Fort when word was brought of the Mexican-Indian revolt led by Tomas Romero and Pablo Montoya; a revolt that brought death to the first American governor of New Mexico (and Wootton's friend and adviser) Charles Bent. Uncle Dick quickly gathered a handful of his fellow trappers and headed south across the freezing Colorado plains.

The men realized that they couldn't possibly put down the revolt by themselves but they felt they could at least avenge the deaths of such men as Bent, Prefect Cornelio Vigil and Circuit Attorney James Leal. Where vengeance was concerned they were primarily interested in running to ground the killers of the owner and operator of Turley's Still in Arroyo Hondo. It might be all right to kill a few politicians, but putting the world's best source of Taos Lightening out of business was carrying things a bit too far.

The mountain men, along with Ceran St. Vrain were in the van after joining with regular forces in pursuit of the rebels. When the last of the insurgents, led by a huge Delaware known as Big Nigger, were cornered in a church near Taos, they were put to the sword. All, that is, except Big Nigger and two or three other Delawares who escaped into the nearby mountains. After the way the Delawares had fought in the church, no one bothered to go into the mountains hunting for Big Nigger. It was felt that the reward placed on his head was entirely too small for the risk involved.

When New Mexico once again relatively peaceful, Wootton began to cast about for some way to turn a quick dollar. He decided that he might make a little sheep drive. Just a little one, from Taos to Sacramento, California, where he was sure the gold miners would welcome a change in their diet. So, in 1852 he hired thirty one drovers, bought 14,000 virtually worthless (in the Taos area) sheep and drove them to California.

The trip took a hundred and seven days, across seemingly endless salt flats, over and through the mountains, past the ever watchful eyes of the Ute and Apache warriors, none of whom were too fond of sheep and harbored a certain natural resentment to their being driven across their land. Wootton, in his account of the trip said they lost about two thousand sheep on the way, had a little Indian trouble but "got by alright."

In Sacramento Wootton sold the sheep that remained for $8.75 a head, paid off the drovers and wound up with forty thousand dollars to take back to New Mexico. He bought some pack animals and some green hides and was ready to go. He placed the money in the tail end of each hide, which, as it dried, formed a perfect pocket for the money. According to Wootton,

"It took a lot of hides and a lot of mules, but it worked."

The return trip took thirty-eight days but with the money safe in hand, it allowed Dick time to plan for the future. He settled on ranching, establishing his range along Huerfano Creek. The ranch was supposed to deal in domesticated buffalos, but Wootton soon turned his talents to other fields. The buffalo could be tamed but no one ever found out quite what to do with one after they tamed it. The enterprise never really got off the ground. With Wootton's acknowledged ability with a dollar, it can be assumed that he found someone who wasn't familiar with the tame buffalo market and unloaded both the ranch and the buffalo for a profit. Uncle Dick turned then to freighting, leaving the long hauls to others and operating exclusively in the eastern Colorado-northeastern New Mexico area, soon landing an Army contract freighting for Fort Union.

The army contract called for so many dollars for so many tons over so many miles. Wootton questioned some of the mileages used by the Quartermaster Corps on the haul from Fort Union to Santa Fe, said to be one hundred and sixty miles. Uncle Dick was convinced that it was farther than that and succeeded finally in having a new survey made of the route. Sure enough, it turned out to be a fraction over one hundred and sixty two miles. Wotton was paid on the basis of the newly established mileage.

Few people ever messed with Dick Wootton. He was equally ready to fight the New Mexico rebels, Indians or the U.S. Army. He was instrumental in the rescue of New Mexico land baron Lucien Maxwell when Maxwell and his party were beset by a band of unfriendly Utes. He also singlehandedly put down a strike by forty of his teamsters who felt that the discipline on a Wootton train was too severe. Wootton held off the teamsters through a day and a night of obviously ineffectual shooting on the part of the disgruntled employees. When the smoke had cleared there were no longer forty teamsters able to work. Those who could returned to their old jobs without a murmur.

Another indication of his fierce competitiveness where the property and-or life of Wootton was concerned came about when a band of thieves from the village of La Palazarita, who were in the habit of preying on the wagon trains that stopped at the fort to rest and repair their equipment decided to try their luck with a Wootton train. Wootton had ignored the problems as long as the thieves left his gear alone. One night they took a Wootton wagon, complete with team. Wootton and a couple of friends rode over to the village, picked up a suspect and led him to a nearby cottonwood with en eye on a quick trial.

As the suspect pleaded his innocence, even ignorance of the foul crime, Wootton placed a noose around his neck and proceeded to lift him from the ground. With his memory amazingly refreshed, the suspect assured Wootton that if he were freed he would see that the guilty persons returned the stolen items and that Wootton equipment would never again be bothered. It turned out that he spoke the truth. The wagon and team were returned and Wootton never again bothered by the La Palazarita bandits.

Wootton became a legend in his own time on Christmas Eve, 1858. Although the deed was accomplished mostly because of the strong profit motive that was part of the Wootton character, he virtually saved the struggling community on Cherry Creek known as Denver. Denver's residents at the time were nearly all miners and mostly tenderfeet. An improvident group, they seldom planned ahead. They hadn't thought, for example, about laying in a supply of food for the winter and had apparently given no thought whatsoever to the fact that wagon trains stopped when blizzards hit the high plains.

It was bad enough that they had run out of canned goods, but now they were even out of the basic necessities of a miner's life: flour and whiskey. Most of them might have been able to make it even without bread, but most would surely die of thirst before the spring thaw. With the prospect of a dry (and hungry) Christmas the populace was overjoyed when over the frozen prairie there appeared four wagons, led by Uncle Dick Wootton.

Three of the wagons were loaded with food but the other was loaded to the bows with Taos Lightening, mother's milk to the pick and shovel men. Uncle Dick had turned what might have been a totally cheerless Christmas into a real celebration. Needless to say, he was still selling flour when even the hangovers had been forgotten.

Having become a local civic leader overnight, Wootton and his wife were invited to settle down in the Cherry Creek diggings and open a trading store. They gave the teamster a quarter section of land in what is now the heart of downtown Denver where Wootton promptly erected a building and opened for business. The building was too large for immediate needs, so one room was rented to a couple of itinerant printers named Byers and Gibson. Wootton helped the two print the first edition of "The Rocky Mountain News."

Feeling that Denver would never amount to much (no one is always right) Wootton sold his holdings and headed south, casting about for something that would support him in his old age. He knew that buffalo ranching was no good, that the time was past to make a killing in the fur trade business; he obviously had no head for real estate operations, so he drew on his long experience in freighting turning his thought to the possibility of a road across the pass at Raton.

Wootton entered into a deal with his old friends the Maxwells, who owned nearly all of northeastern New Mexico, and bought twenty-five hundred acres of land along Raton and Gallinas Creeks which just happened to include the pass over the eastward jutting arm of the Sangre de Cristo mountains that included the pass.

The route was used by every traveler from either north or south, going to or coming from Santa Fe and the states. The easier although sometimes more dangerous Cimarron Cut Off had been made virtually unusable by the Kiowa and Comanche, who had returned to the plains in strength during the Civil War while the white man was busy killing his own kind.

Wootton had not only a built in market for his road, but the courage and reputation to make a toll for the use of the road stick. With a charter from the legislatures of Colorado and New Mexico he set out to build a road over the nearly eight thousand foot pass. How good a road was not specified but anyone who wanted to use it would pay for the privilege. The only exceptions were Indians and posses chasing horse thieves. The former because Wootton figured they had prior claim, the latter because they wouldn't have the time to stop.

After smoothing off the rough spots and removing the larger stumps and boulders, Wootton put a chain across the path and set up a tariff for its use. A wagon could cross the pass for a dollar fifty; a horse and rider, twenty five cents; Livestock crossed for a nickel a head, Wootton count. When the county commissioners of Las Animas County, Colorado, felt that Wootton was making too much money, they forced him to lower his rates. Wootton promptly countered by raising it on the New Mexico end.

To help promote a little more business and to make a few extra dollars, Uncle Dick established a road house in conjunction with his toll house, offering the traveler food and drink, a bed, and on Saturday nights a place to dance. It soon became the most popular night spot in the county for the youngbloods from Trinidad. On a good day Uncle Dick would take in four to five hundred dollars from the combined operation.

There was a dance in progress on a cold night in February, 1878 when Uncle Dick was called from the roadhouse to meet a stranger. The man, bundled in heavy clothing against the cold winter air of the pass, introduced himself as A.A. Robinson, a surveyor for the Santa Fe railroad. He had, he said, a proposition for Uncle Dick.

It seemed that the Santa Fe had built to Pueblo and run short of money. Knowing that they would be stymied if they didn't move either south or west, they had engaged in a losing battle with General Palmer's Denver & Rio Grande for trackage rights through the Royal Gorge and entry into the lush San Luis Valley. Now they were racing against both time and the Rio Grande for an outlet to the markets of the southwest and eventually the Pacific coast.

Robinson and his fellow engineers, Ray Morley, Lew Kingman and Will Strong had persuaded the Santa Fe home office to let them move south and try to make a deal for a route through Raton from the junction at La Junta. Permission was finally granted, but the men were warned that no more than twenty thousand dollars would be available for the survey work and it would be nice if they didn't have to spend anything at all.

In the cloak and dagger atmosphere of late nineteenth century big business, Robinson and his crew had boarded the Rio Grande train in Pueblo headed for Trinidad, coat collars turned up, faces buried in their newspapers to escape recognition. At Trinidad they rented a rig and headed up the pass to Wootton's toll house, hoping that they might convince him to sell the Santa Fe the right of way through the gap in the mountains.

Since the only competition for the route was Palmer's line, Uncle Dick was easily convinced. Palmer's somewhat high handed methods had alienated a large portion of the population.

Wootton roused the sleeping teamsters and emptied the dance hall, offering work on the railroad.

"It ain't the Rio Grande, is it?" his guests asked.

"No," Wootton told them, "this is for the Santa Fe . . . a chance to put that Springs millionaire in his place."

Picks and shovels were supplied and the Santa Fe started their grade through the pass in the freezing mountain night by the light of candles and lanterns. Under the laws of the day, stakes and grade work, no matter how little, gave the Santa Fe prior right to the use of the route.

Although Robinson had offered Uncle Dick fifty thousand dollars that the line didn't have for the right of way, Wootton refused. He maintained a lump sum of that size was too hard to handle. He settled for a lifetime pass on the line for he and his wife and twenty-five dollars a month (also for life) in groceries. The grateful Santa Fe, in recognition of his help, named the first consolidated type locomotive on the line, specifically built for the Trinidad-Raton run, "the Uncle Dick."

The old man lived out his life on a thousand acre ranch near the summit of the pass, in full view of one of the first landmarks he had seen when he came west as a youth, Castle Rock. He claimed, with some justice, that he had done his bit to populate the west. Married four times he fathered twenty children of whom twelve were alive at his death. His eyesight failed in later years and although he travelled to Chicago for help, his vision was too far gone. Uncle Dick, mountain man and business man, a rare combination, finished his years in darkness, dying August 21, 1893, a wanderer and explorer who managed to make a buck in the process.

UNCLE DICK in trapper's outfit. Photo—Colorado Historical Society.

WOOTTON RANCH near the crest of the pass where the old man spent his declining years. Photo—AT&SF Ry.

THE "UNCLE DICK" built specifically for the grades over the pass at Raton and named for the old trapper who gave the railroad its much sought after outlet to the west. The engine was a Baldwin compound with saddle tanks. Photo—AT&SF Ry.

SANTA FE'S Number One, the C.K. Holliday as restored in the line's Topeka shops. Locomotives like the Uncle Dick replaced the little 2-4-0's on the heavier mountain runs. Photo—AT&SF Ry.

MOUNTAINS A-ROUND Raton are filled with the residue of history. This burned out ranch house stands a lonely vigil in the bare hills above the town.

FORT UNION from the hill, as it appeared in the days when Wootton held the military freighting contract. Photo—Colorado Historical Society.

LITTLE IS LEFT of Fort Union but crumbling adobe corners and the more substantially built guardhouse.

OFFICER'S ROW, Fort Union, N.M.

PARADE GROUND, Fort Union.

FORT UNION may have lacked creature comforts but the esthetics were fine. The snow capped Sangre de Cristos are seen through what was once a window in the post hospital.

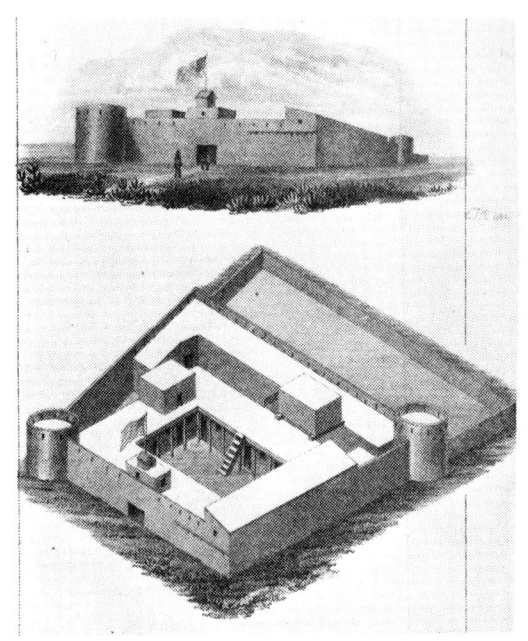

BENT'S FORT on the Arkansas was Uncle Dick's first western home. He served as a trapper, a trader, a hunter and a wagon boss for the firm of Bent and St. Vrain before striking out on his own. Photo—Colorado Historical Society.

UNCLE DICK'S combination road house, toll house and hotel on the Colorado end of his toll road. Building was a social center for residents of the northern end of the road. Photo—Colorado Historical Society.

5 *The Coward Killer Meets His End*

The walls of the narrow canyon seemed to shake as the shotgun blast filled the street with a shock wave of sound. A woman screamed hysterically as the citizens of Creede splashed through the muddy streets to the tent saloon. On the floor lay the crumpled body of what had been a tall, slightly built man, his blood puddling in the sawdust slightly staining the brim of what had been his trademark, the biggest hat west of the Mississippi.

At the door of the temporary gambling palace stood a grubby, sandy haired man, Ed Kelly, a Hinsdale County deputy sheriff and currently the marshal of nearby Bachelor Camp. He held a twelve gauge shotgun, still smoking, in his hand as though he expected his victim to rise and return the fire. Kelly was a loser and a stranger wherever he went: a man who would in his own turn, die by gunfire on the streets of Oklahoma City, his only claim to fame having been the killing of the killer of Jesse James, Bob Ford.

Ed Kelly had more names than he did reputation. He was referred to variously as Kelly, O'Kelly and as Red, Jim and Ed. He had little in the way of a past and his future looked just as bleak. He had, according to most reports, come from the hills of Missouri where he was described as having been either a distant relative of the James brothers or one of the many fringe members of the James gang.

In the mid eighties Kelly had drifted into Colorado with the influx of gold and silver seekers. He was one of those people in the early west who worked only as a last resort, sometimes as a marshal if the town were hard up enough for some to wear a badge. The rest of the time they hung around the bars and the gambling tables, riding the grub line when their stake ran out. Kelly, so far as is known, never held a regular job.

Ford and Kelly had crossed paths frequently in the gold rush towns, having known each other in both Pueblo and Walsenburg. Ed gained some fame as a bad man on the eastern slope, reportedly having killed four men, although the only provable killing was that of an unfortunate black, one Ed Rilley who lost his life as a result of stepping on Kelly's feet in a Pueblo saloon.

Kelly and his only friend, French Joe Duval, had crossed the mountains from Walsenburg when they heard about the strike in Willow Creek canyon. They weren't looking for a bonanza of their own, but just wanted to be where the action was, hoping of course, that someone else's luck might find its way into the Kelly and Duval pockets. They wound up in Creede, the only place in the canyon that really qualified as a town. It was run by the master their and con artist, Jefferson "Soapy" Smith, who included in his entourage of fast talkers and crooked dealers, the "dirty little coward who shot Mr. Howard," Bob Ford.

Ford had a less than likeable reputation even among the minions of the ubquitous Smith. He was said to be the loudest mouthed, cockiest and most obnoxious of the lot and his conceit in the area of feminine conquests was unbearable. In Creede he was keeping house in his fancy two story Exchange with Nell Watson who was in charge of the second floor (and the girls) of the combination house of ill repute-dance hall-gambling palace-saloon.

Ford hadn't really had a comfortable day since the killing, ten years before in 1882, of Jesse James. He was never seen on the street without a rifle and always, shades of Wild Bill Hickock, sat with his back to a wall. The sound of the song about poor Jesse's wife being a widow and a mourner all her life sent him into a frenzy, more of fright than anger. He became particularly incensed when he was referred to as a dirty little coward who had taken unfair advantage of an almost simon pure train and bank robber, thereby causing Mr. Howard to be laid in his grave. A letter addressed to Frank James once came to Creede which put Ford into both shock and hiding. Fortunately no one ever claimed the letter, which led Ford to brag even more loudly of his prowess with a gun.

Kelly, on the other hand, had to make do without the sponsorship of Smith. On his arrival he took the job as marshal of Bachelor Camp, which automatically made him an unpaid deputy sheriff. The job at Bachelor must not have been too onerous since he appears to have spent most of his time in nearby Creede with the card and bottle set. Aside from Duval and Ford hardly anyone seemed to know or care to know Kelly. About the only notice he received was the result of a fight in the Orleans Saloon in February of 1892. Because of the fight he was ordered to leave town by as unlikely a pair of town marshals as one could imagine, Soapy Smith and Bat Masterson.

Despite the orders of what passed for law in Creede, Kelly felt that it was too early to go home, so he wandered over to Ford's Exchange. Once again he ran afoul of the law and order folks. He got into an argument with Ford, whereupon Bob and his bouncer, aided by some excellent licks with the bung starter, tossed the marshal of Bachelor into the street. Thoughtfully they had removed his gun just in case he might harbor some thought of immediate revenge for this treatment. Kelly returned to his shack in the canyon considerably miffed at the treatment he had received in the big town.

Creede rocked along as calmly as any boom camp could until the night of June 4th, 1892 when it was struck with that common mining town disaster, fire. The flames wiped out one side of the street putting Ford and numerous other purveyors of booze and girls out of business temporarily. Ford reopened in a tent June 6th but the event was spoiled by the suicide death of one of Nell's girls.

Bob, always a real sport, was quite bitter about both the girl and her timing as he went about town taking up a collection to help pay for her funeral. His requests for funds were, as a rule, so backhanded that several people suggested that he might be better off back at the saloon leaving the charitable works to those better suited for that type of thing.

Kelly was among the crowd of curiousity seekers who swarmed into town to see and in some cases help repair the damage, although Ed gave little thought to being helpful. With all of the confusion Kelly decided that now might be a good time to square accounts with Ford. But before he could even get up a good head of steam for revenge for the last indignities, he had additional cause for a grudge.

He climbed the steps to the tent that had replaced the far more imposing Exchange and asked the bartender if he happened to know where Ford could be found. The bartender inquired as to Kelly's business and was told that Ed was an old friend from Missouri. Ford, as all the help knew, had very friends anywhere and none of them happened to be from Missouri. The barkeep signalled the bouncer, pulled a shotgun from under the bar and Kelly was on his way to the street again.

While the bartender covered Kelly, the bouncer belted him around a few times, once again taking Kelly's gun, thereby exploding at least one myth; that of the fearless westerner never giving up his weapon. Then the two of them took Kelly to the door and tossed him down the steps and into the muddy street once again.

Now Kelly was beginning to get mad. It appeared that every time he came to town either someone took his gun and beat him up or asked him to leave. Upset by this turn of events he crossed over to the Major Mercantile House and bought himself another pistol, thereby establishing himself as one of that firm's better firearm customers.

With his old buddy French Joe Duval he spent the balance of the day drinking courage and planning not only revenge but the reattainment of his self respect as well. He was, after all, a bad man and bad men had their fans and reputation to consider. And aside from the revenge, Kelly felt that he could perhaps add even more luster to his somewhat tarnished reputation by becoming the man who avenged the death of good old Jesse.

Late the morning of June 8th, Kelly set out to find Ford, although the route he took indicated that he was not hunting too hard for the rifle wielding killer. He started his search at the Holy Moses but bartender Jim Osgood informed him that Ford had not been in. Back on the street he nodded to French Joe who was patiently waiting on a horse with a shotgun across the saddle. Kelly, with Duval following, went to the Leadville Club but still no Ford. In and out of the saloons Kelly trudged, French Joe keeping pace and watching the street for any sign of Ford.

They finally made it to the one place where Ford was bound to appear sometime during the day, his own Exchange. Kelly saw his victim going up the steps and into the tent. Hurriedly he called French Joe who met him in front of the Tortoni Hotel and handed him the shotgun.

Running across the street and up the steps Kelly kept his target in sight. As he went in the front of the saloon he saw Ford headed for the raised platform in the rear which held the enclosed section of the saloon housing living quarters and the office.

"Hello, Bob," said Kelly, speaking the last words Ford would ever hear.

Always ready for the trouble he was sure to come Ford spun and started to raise his rifle. Kelly fired both the duck shot filled barrels, catching Ford in the throat. The bouncer and the bartender dived behind the bar as Nell came running from the platform. When she saw Ford lying in an ever widening pool of blood she began to scream, bringing deputies Plunkett and Rosen on the run.

The deputies immediately disarmed Kelly and turned to protect him from the crowd when Kelly uttered one of the most cryptic remarks in the annals of western literature.

"I don't burn a man's mother's heels," he said with an obvious flair for the poetic, "and I don't rob pocketbooks, or pull toenails with pincers, but I can kill a low down murderer like Bob Ford."

The exact meaning of the statement, since they had nothing on Kelly for heel burning or toenail pulling, but rather a murder, seemed to escape the arresting officers and Sheriff Gardner who was now on the scene.

"What do you mean," asked the sheriff?

"I've said all I'm going to say," answered Kelly, which was probably just as well if all his statements were going to be in the same vein.

As Kelly was led away, the faithful Nell vocally mourned the loss of a staunch civic leader like Ford, cut down in his prime, according to Nell, as he went about trying to do good for his fellow man. Ford, Nell said, wouldn't have drawn a shotgun on a coyote, but rather would have faced it out with pistols at some reasonable range, like two miles. Nell apparently had forgotten about the rifle that was Ford's constant companion when on the street. When Nell commented that Ford was a good fellow, one of the reporters for the Creede Chronicle was heard to remark that she was right, now.

Kelly was led off to a small house in south Creede that was serving as the local jail. The mob that followed the officers was growing larger and meaner when good old Soapy Smith arrived on the scene. Smith, in his best Victorian oratorical style urged the crowd to let the law handle people like Kelly. Law and order prevailed, fortunately for the prisoner. To give Soapy his due, he averted the lynching, but his reasons probably weren't totally unselfish. Soapy felt that a lynching would bring more real law to Creede than the Smith gang could stand.

Ford's funeral was the social highlight of the summer for Creede. The body, borne to the hillside cemetery in a wagon rented from Braiden's Livery Stable, led a procession more than a mile in length. In the van was a weeping Nell, accompanied by the girls who had worked upstairs in the Exchange.

Kelly, true to form, turned out to have guessed wrong again. Instead of being proclaimed a hero and public benefactor, he became the town heel. Most of the citizens of Creede, it turned out, cared little about the memory of Jesse James and even less about old family feuds in Missouri. Even French Joe, feeling the public pulse, decided that he would do better elsewhere. Those folks in Colorado could have cared less about the code of the mountains.

Kelly was tried in Lake City and sentenced to either life or ninety nine years, depending upon whose account you read, on July 12, 1892. To some segments of the population, Jesse James aside, the sentence seemed a bit too long for killing any member of Soápy Smith's gang; some even considered it a public service. Efforts were immediately started on Kelly's behalf to have him either freed or the sentence reduced. They had some success. First the sentence was reduced to eighteen years, then, after ten years, Kelly was pardoned for doing away with Bob Ford.

After his release from the state hotel at Canyon City, Kelly dropped out of sight for a year, then reappears in the then young Oklahoma City. He still kept company with an unsavory lot; Marvin and Guy Terney from Iowa, Jerome Calhoun, a real gun nut who kept an arsenal in his room on West Main and the weirdest of the bunch, Bob Jackson, whose major business and interest was holding up sporting houses.

By now Kelly had some feeling of kinship with Ford, and no matter the weather he always wore an overcoat, a miserable habit during most of the year in Oklahoma City. In the overcoat and on his person he carried three guns and two knives, which should have given him at least a small feeling of security. The Oklahoma City Times noted in his obituary that Kelly hung out with other loafers and bums in the notorious saloons along First Street, only removing his hands from his pockets long enough to lift a few with his friends.

Officer Bunker first put the arm on Kelly, catching him leaving a saloon in December 1903 with his overcoat over his arm. Bunker ran Kelly in for vagrancy but the charge failed to stick. On release Kelly swore that no one would ever arrest him again.

On the bitter cold night of January 14th, 1904 the police were looking for one of Ed's friends, Bob Jackson. It seems that Lillian Johnson's house on Second Street had been robbed and naturally the prime suspect was Jackson. About nine in the evening, patrolman Joseph Burnett saw Kelly and two companions in the 200 block of West First and approached him for questioning, not arrest. Coming up from behind, Burnett called,

"Hello, Kelly."

Kelly turned and drew a gun from his ample supply, shouting,

"I'll arrest you, you S.O.B."

Kelly raised his gun and struck at the officer but Burnett caught the weapon and held it away. Kelly's companions fired two errant shots in the general direction of the policeman then took to their heels with Kelly shouting all the while for them to stay and help him "murder this fellow."

The officer and the killer struggled for the better part of fifteen minutes while Ed called for his departed comrades and Burnett looked about for help. The fight was witnessed by the tower operator of the local street railway but he was too busy to leave his post. He did report, however, that another officer who had been on the other side of First when the battle began had left the scene on a dead run when the shots were fired.

As they battled up and down the street, Kelly kept trying to bring his pistol to bear but met with little success. A later examination of Burnett by City Physician Witten disclosed the total damage to the officer was one powder burned ear, one well chewed ear and two bullet holes in his coat.

Burnett finally got some help when a Frisco baggageman named Paul, having heard the sounds of battle, ran the two blocks from the depot and grabbed Kelly. Burnett then drew his own gun and without the formality of reading Kelly his rights, fired twice, Kelly falling lifeless to the ground.

The body was taken to Street and Harper's Funeral Home followed by the customary gaggle of curious onlookers who crowded into the street as soon as the fight was over. Both of the officer's shots had hit his assailant, one shattering his left knee, the other and fatal shot having entered his left temple and emerged from behind his right ear. The funeral home was swamped the rest of the night by the morbidly curious coming to view the remains.

Kelly's companions were arrested in their rooming house and asked about the array of guns that were found there. All assured the officers that they were avid sportsmen and hunters who had come to Oklahoma in search of the elusive prairie chicken. They were released after they promised to hunt the prairie chicken elsewhere.

Kelly's death was front page news but his funeral, held on the sixteenth, rated barely a notice from either the paper or the residents of Oklahoma City, He was buried, not with a mile of mourners, but virtually alone. There was no weeping or wailing at the loss of the man who had killed the killer of Jesse James. The newspaper even pointed out that Kelly had "gotten his just deserts and the right man won" in the shoot out on First Street.

The life of a man who had planned to become a hero by killing a murderer and acknowledged coward ended on the frozen streets of Oklahoma City; done in by an ordinary policeman and a baggagemen whose last name has been lost to history; deserted by his alleged friends, unmourned and missed by no one.

ONE MINE is still active enough in Willow Creek to require the services of the Rio Grande branch line that dead ends at Creede.

STREET SCENE, Creede, Colorado, 1892. Photo—Colorado Historical Society.

BOB FORD, *killer of Jesse James, went more than a little paranoid when he heard the then popular song about Jesse being laid in his grave. Photo—Colorado Historical Society.*

TRUST A GOOD *shooting to draw a crowd, even the kids who were supposed to be in school. This was taken in front of the Exchange shortly after Ford was cut down by Kelly's shotgun. Photo—Colorado Historical Society.*

ABANDONED HEAD WORKS dot the hills above modern Creede. Signs indicate that whoever the present owner might be, he doesn't want curiousity seekers anywhere around the premises.

THERE IS STILL a little mining activity in Willow Creek canyon, although most of the active mines have long since been abandoned to vandals who have stripped them of everything of value.

ABOUT THE ONLY picture Kelly ever sat for was this one with a number on his chest taken by the State of Colorado while Kelly was its guest in Canyon City. Photo— Denver Public Library.

WILLOW CREEK CANYON, where old man Creede's Holy Moses mine opened yet another new field for the inveterate gold seekers.

CREEDE WAS, of necessity, a one street town confined between the nearly sheer walls of Willow Creek canyon. This view is from 1892, the year Ford met his end. Photo—Denver Public Library.

FORD'S FUNERAL was more than a mile long, led by his weeping lady friend, Nell Watson. Photo—Colorado Historical Society.

 ## The Texans Are Coming

Harness jingling, the Buckskin Joe stage jolted heavily over the dry midsummer ruts as it approached the McLaughlin Ranch, homeward bound on its weekly run through the mining camps west of Denver.

Although elsewhere in the country this July of 1864 the sound of bugles and cannons could be heard, this had been the usual uneventful trip for driver Al Williamson and superintendent Billy McClelland. The route, from Denver to Breckenridge, Fairplay, then back through Alma and Hamilton to Denver might as well have been on another planet, the battle between the forces of the north and south seemed so far away.

It was a light trip for the express box, too, with only about three thousand in dust and amalgam from the Orphan Boy mine and whatever of value might be in the two mailsacks riding in the boot. All in all, the stage seemed as unlikely a target for robbery as the driver and his boss were ever apt to see. And they certainly didn't expect to be braced by a motley group of self styled Confederate soldiers, raiding for the cause a thousand miles from the war.

As they reined in to the McLaughlin Ranch some two miles south of Hamilton and prepared to dismount, they were accosted by nine heavily armed, obviously serious and perhaps dangerous men, some of whom had built a reputation for toughness in South Park before the war.

"Throw up your hands," came the order from the leader, an old time South Park tough, Jim Reynolds.

"I don't know why you would want to rob me," replied Williamson. "Everybody knows that a stage driver never has any money."

With that he handed the robbers the fifteen cents he had on his person.

The bandits, or irregulars, or soldiers, depending on their state of sobriety did better with McClelland, relieving him of four hundred dollars, a gold watch and a revolver. Lifting the strong box from the stage, Reynolds told one of his men to fetch an axe.

"No need for that, Jim," the driver said, "I have the key right here."

"What kind of robber would use a key?" asked Reynolds, a man with an obvious flair for both propriety and dramatics. "Give me the axe and we'll bust this box the right way."

Taking the axe, he dealt the box a blow, breaking the hasp. Dumping the amalgam and dust on the ground, he handed the axe to one of his followers, telling him to break the stage wheel spokes in the hope of slowing pursuit. Taking the stage horses (Reynolds seemed incapable of leaving an unattended horse anywhere) the nine so-called Confederates rode rapidly into the hills.

The robbery of the Buckskin Joe stage was the first indication the citizens of Colorado had that they were to be invaded. Not, as it turned out, by an army, but by some of the more larcenous types ever to cloak their activities under the guise of a military campaign.

With three thousand in gold and five thousand in currency from the mail sacks, the band rode off toward Denver, there to either rout the federals or rob the banks, whichever seemed the most appropriate at the time. With only nine men they looked considerably more like highwaymen than a military expedition.

Jim Reynolds, the leader, was not riding strange ground, having come to the South Park region in the late 1850's to make his fortune one way or another. He had settled at Fairplay in the early days of the camp and had become something of a leader (and a minor league Soapy Smith) through physical strength and his ability with a gun. The ability was, not incidentally, coupled with a readiness to use it as well.

Although Reynolds was the leader of the only known band of guerillas to enter Colorado during the Civil War, his was not the only group to undertake the capture of the territory for the greater glory of the South. The first threat came from a bunch of more or less home grown rebels, including Reynolds. Men already in Colorado but with definite southern sympathies.

Jim, along with his brother John had joined the forces of Captain McKee of Geneva Gulch during the summer of 1861. John McKee, the leader, has been described as a man of some ambition who had made a strike in the Gulch. He had been holding small meetings each night in the camps, recruiting men for the war he was sure would come to Colorado.

McKee must have been a better prospector than he was a tactitian. Out of his own pocket he armed, outfitted and mounted a small band intending, once battle was joined, to sack Denver, Leadville, Pueblo and Santa Fe while riding south to link up with the regular forces.

That old devil Loose Lip proved to be the undoing of McKee's army. Strict secrecy had been the Captain's order, but word reached Denver that McKee was preparing to move. The army, all seventy of them, were surprised by Federal troops, disarmed and locked up in the open pen that served at that time as the Denver jail.

The rebels were not the only ones with problems, although being kept in the open day and night would indicate to the casual observer that their's were the worst. It took all of the First Colorado Volunteers to guard the prisoners while General Carlton, off in New Mexico to repel the rebels under General Sibley was keeping the dispatch riders hot asking Governor Gilpin for more troops, a relatively common failing shared by Union generals throughout the conflict.

The only troops available were busy guarding a rag tag bunch of miners and bartenders, so Governor Gilpin made arrangements to let the prisoners escape, feeling that on their record, they weren't as much of a threat to the Union free as they were in jail.

One evening the guards failed to show up, only an officer who took great pains to let the prisoners know that the gate had somehow been left unlocked. Even Captain McKee understood that escape was possible and pursuit unlikely so the Captain and his gallant band silently stole from the cage, through the streets of Denver and headed south.

The irregulars made their way south to Texas where Reynolds whiled away his time planning a return to Colorado (and the gold fields) hoping to become a second Quantrell, which should give some insight into the Reynolds personality. He placed his plan in front of McKee, now on active service with the Confederates. McKee authorized Reynolds to raise a band of mounted men under the command of Reynolds, to go north and empty Colorado.

The raiders were ready to go in April of 1864. Rallying around Reynolds were only twenty two men, apparently the only ones in that part of Texas with enough larceny in their souls to attempt a twelve hundred mile ride (one way) through the worst Indian country in the world to what could not be imagined as a friendly reception by those they planned to victimize.

Reynolds, ever the optimist, felt sure that he could pick up recruits along the way and invited McKee to accompany the raid and share in the glory and the loot. McKee had had enough of the open air Denver jail so he demurred. He did, however, arrange passage for Reynolds and his troop through the lines at Belknap.

Reynolds' men were better prepared to fight than they were to travel. Aside from a brush with some wandering Cheyennes the trip was uneventful. Uneventful, that is, if you consider being on the verge of starvation as a mundane thing. It seems that Reynolds had neglected to recruit a quartermaster so as they approached the southeast corner of Colorado they were reduced to eating their pack mules.

An accidental meeting with a Mexican pack train near Spanish Peaks led to their first success against the Yankees, although the poor drovers probably had no idea that they were being killed for any cause more noble than their cargos, animals and supplies. The pack yielded some forty eight thousand dollars in coin, drafts and currency and led to the first breach in the ranks of the raiders.

Reynolds held that since he was the leader and had been responsible for all of the expense of the expedition to date, he would look after the money until such time as they could conveniently split it up. Some of the patriots felt that now was as good a time as any. Reynolds held to his original stand with the result that fourteen of the stout hearted Confederates quit on the spot and headed for home where they could keep whatever they could steal.

The gang was thus reduced to the leader, Jim Reynolds, his brother, John, Jack Robinson, Tom Knight, Owen Singleterry, John Babbitt, Jake Stowe, John Andrews and Tom Hallinam. Not a very large force with which to take Colorado but by then their aims had been reduced; now all they really had in mind to do was steal everything they could carry and retire to a life of ease.

Caching the heavy coin and some extra weapons on the Arkansas near Pueblo the raiders headed west. Camping near Canyon City they bought food, clothing and whiskey at Bradley's Store then headed for Current Creek to rest and lay their plans. It might be noted that Bradley was running in luck; this was the last time they paid for anything.

Breaking up in groups of three they rode from Current Creek for California Gulch, to met near Fairplay Sunday, July 24th, 1864 at

Guireaud's Ranch. After a couple of meals and a night's lodging they decided they might as well rob the inbound Buckskin stage just to get in practice. To repay Guireaud for his hospitality they departed from habit and custom and refrained from stealing any of his horses.

Crossing a small creek below the McLaughlin Ranch they met the station manager, McLaughlin and Major De Mary (or, as some have it, Demere) manager of the Phillips mine. Leaving De Mary, described as a "portly, middle aged" man to contemplate his fate, the riders concentrated on McLaughlin, inquiring first as to the expected time of arrival of the stage, then asking about the possibility of a trade for the fine horse he was riding.

McLaughlin told them he was not in a trading mood, but the sudden appearance of guns in every hand gave him a sudden change of heart and a deal was struck. Major De Mary, known to Reynolds, was looked upon as a veritable golden goose. He was known to hide the product of the mine in the most unlikely places, so it was assumed that he probably had some on his person. Such was not the case. When the goose was shaken he yielded only a hundred dollars and an excellent hat that struck the fancy of one of the raiders.

The bad men had a wait before the stage was due so they imposed on the manager for some whiskey and a meal. Apparently they drank more than they ate because Reynolds was soon confiding in his two prisoners. The riders they saw were, Reynolds said, just the vanguard of fifteen hundred Texas troops bound for Colorado.

While Reynolds and his by now merry men entertained McLaughlin and De Mary with fanciful tales, an unnoticed and unwilling eavesdropper grew wide eyed. A newsbutcher by the name of Berry was resting at the ranch when the bandits appeared. The more he heard the more Berry felt that he must spread the alarm as soon as it was safe for him to leave.

Immediately after the robbers had cleaned the stage and left, Berry mounted and raced toward Denver to arouse the settlers and warn them to flee for their lives and hide the livestock. The warning about the stock was particularly appropriate. The Reynolds mob had a penchant for fresh horseflesh; a habit that was, in time, to spell doom for some of the band.

The adventures of the newsbutcher Berry as he headed east would make a delightful fairy tale. At times he was behind the invaders and sometimes he was ahead of them. At one point he and a saddle companion, Charles Hall, were guests of the Reynolds men at dinner in one of the stage stops. When Berry was queried by Reynolds about the prospects in Denver, he assured him that no self respecting bandit would even set foot in the place, things were so dull.

Berry eventually reached Denver on the 26th where his hue and cry was generally ignored. General David Cook, former Denver city marshal finally put the wheels in motion for a military posse and sure enough, in only thirty hours such a posse under the command of Captain Maynard leisurely set out to do the road agents in.

By then the country was swarming with posses possessing varying degrees of enthusiasm. They were so thick that Reynolds decided that it would be best if he found a safe place for the nearly fifty thousand dollars he had in his saddle bags. Not only were there too many posses, but he was beginning to notice the covetous glances cast his way by his worthy companions.

A posse led by Jack Stark narrowly missed the Reynolds raiders, the bandits turning up Deer Creek just before the twenty possemen thundered down the road on their way to Omaha House, the last reported location of the robbers. Things were getting entirely too warm so Reynolds started casting about for a likely looking hole in which to hide the loot.

Sending the other eight on ahead while he ostensibly was covering the back trail for pursuers, Reynolds went to the head of Elk Creek and found what he considered a likely looking hiding place. There was an old prospect hole just above the swampy headwater meadow that would do the trick just fine. Taking careful note of the lay of the land, Reynolds added a little recognition insurance by breaking off an old butcher knife in the trunk of a nearby tree.

Leaving his private bank Reynolds rejoined his soldiers in a grove of trees in Geneva Gulch, according to some contemporary accounts, or in Platte Canyon according to others. Whichever it was, the camp for the night would be the last the gang would ever share.

The indefatigable Stark was hot on the trail, closing on the camp about dusk on July 31. In the course of a discussion as to whether this was really the bunch they sought, the posse spooked the outlaws, who raced for their horses amid a heavy rain of shot. One, Owen Singleterry, was killed. Jim Reynolds was seriously wounded in the lower arm and four were captured. Singleterry, a nondescript in life became something of a celebrity in death. His head was removed, placed in a jar of alcohol and put on display in Fairplay.

It was the beginning of the end for The Great Confederate Invasion. One by one the men were hunted down, first Hallinam and then the others until all but three had been accounted for by a Lt. Shoup, who, according to his report, ran out of outlaws, food, money and enthusiasm for the chase in Canyon City. He noted in his report that only two of the men, John Reynolds and Jake Stowe, had escaped across the river on a hastily built raft.

Jim Reynolds, his forearm shattered, had struck out alone but his arm gave him such pain that he was forced to turn himself in and seek medical aid in Pueblo. After being treated he was taken once again to Denver where he joined his erstwhile comrades in arms as a prisoner.

The local authorities, one of whom had already said that the bunch should be given a quick, fair trial and then hung, felt that the Denver jail was to insecure for guests of this type so arrangements were made to transfer them to Fort Lyon. A detail commanded by Captain Cree was ordered to escort the prisoners with a more or less tacit understanding that it wouldn't be too terrible if the prisoners never made it. Shot while attempting to escape or something like that would do.

In direct charge of the prisoners was a non com named Aston Shaw. It is not known whether or not he was a super patriot or just trigger happy, but he soon had the one time desperadoes on edge with thinly veiled threats about shooting those who even looked as though they wanted to escape.

The first two nights it was made obvious that escape would be possible, but the prisoners had little heart for the enterprise; they had been on the run long enough. The third day Shaw went to the Captain and said,

"I'm getting almighty tired of herding this bunch of Texans day and night. Something ought to be done about it."

"Very well," answered the Captain, "take who and what you require and get the job done. But don't tell me how it is accomplished."

With official sanction Shaw picked a detail and guided the ambulance in which the prisoners were riding and took it below a bluff on Squirrel Creek. Ordering them to dismount, he lined them up. There is a highly romanticized version of the death of the outlaws, but apparently only Shaw and one other of the guard were willing to serve as executioners.

Reynolds is pictured as dying dead game while his companions begged for their lives. It might even be true, but it would seem odd that the unlettered leader of a group of avowed cutthroats would die quoting an Arthurian vow about living and dying together and their bones bleaching in the desert, an oath that all of them purportedly took before starting the adventure. Oath or no, all but one, John Andrews, who feigned death, died there under the bluff.

On their return to Denver the troopers were greeted with what must have been, at least to Aston, the sad news that while they had been out with a bunch of Texans they had missed out on some great sport at Sand Creek where a bunch of Cheyennes had been given what for. Captain Cree reported that all of the prisoners had escaped and gave the story of flight to the Rocky Mountain News.

Andrews, the survivor, was nursed back to health by a rancher friend, H.N. Cochran. As soon as he had regained his strength he set out for Santa Fe to search out John Reynolds and Jake Stowe. The old comrades, reunited once again, decided to improve their somewhat desperate financial condition by digging up the cache on the Arkansas, but that old urge for just one more horse proved their undoing.

Stopping at a ranch near the New Mexico-Colorado line they were in the process of an unauthorized horse trade when they were surprised by the owners. Showing natural resentment the owners, without even giving them their rights, killed Stowe on the spot and then ran Andrews down in a gully and ended his career as a Confederate soldier, horse trader and sole survivor of a firing squad. John Reynolds escaped again and headed back to Santa Fe to wait for a better time to get the money.

John was the only member of the gang in Jim's confidence when the big money, the nearly fifty thousand dollars was buried. He had given his brother a detailed description of the area, of a horse mired in a swamp, the broken butcher knife in the tree and the prospect hole. John was determined to get the money as soon as the heat had died down a little.

In October of 1871, accompanied by a gambling friend, Al Brown, John Reynolds set out to recover the hard stolen money. He got only as far as Taos when the horse stealing urge caught up with him. Once again the owner objected and mortally wounded the last member of the once feared Reynolds gang.

Brown helped Reynolds to a cave where he might make his last hours easier and also, maybe come up with a map to the big treasure. As Reynolds died, he drew a crude map for Brown so that the money might not go to waste.

With Reynolds dead, Brown traveled to Denver where he struck up an acquaintance with the ubiquitous rancher, Cochran. Together they set out for the Elk Creek hiding place, but found that nature had destroyed all of the recognizable landmarks. A forest fire had burned the tree with the knife blade, landslides had covered the prospect hole and only the skeleton of a horse in the swamp remained. Cochran returned to Denver where he eventually gave the map to General Cook while Brown headed on west to his destiny, death in a Laramie bar room brawl.

Despite the Reynolds boys, Colorado stayed with the Union. The fifteen hundred imaginary soldiers never appeared. In fact, had Reynolds but known, the issue of the Civil War was nearly settled before he and his twenty-two bravos ever left Belknap.

The treasure, if it exists, has never been found. Some say that it never existed except in the imagination of General Cook. But the Reynolds boys got some money, both at Spanish Peaks and the Buckskin hold up. And Jim Reynolds, the bold and bad guerilla put it somewhere. And there it still lays, waiting to be found.

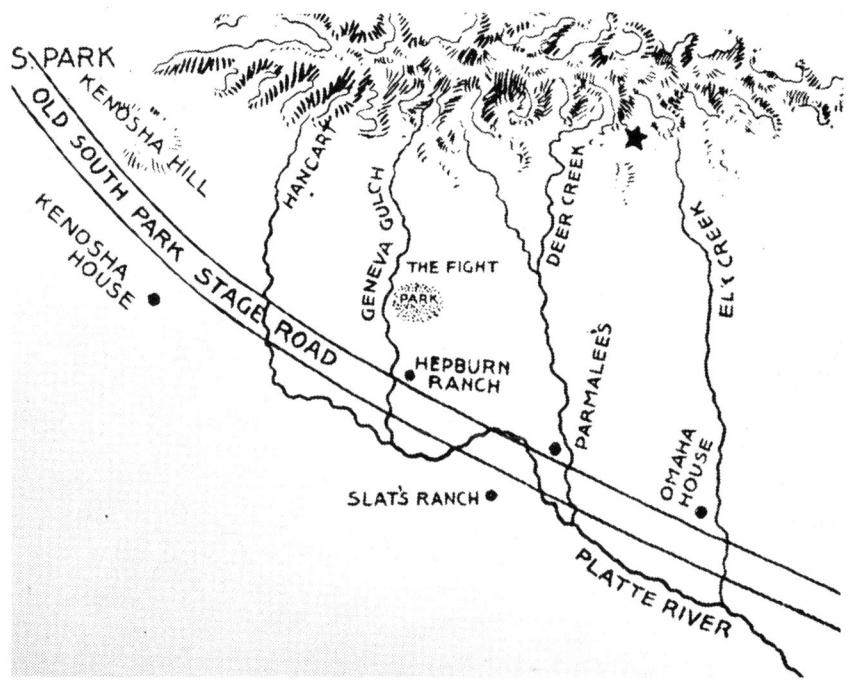

HERE LIES THE TREASURE, provided of course you know where Slat's Ranch is and you can find a tree with a broken butcher knife embedded and the skeleton of a horse. Photo—Denver Public Library.

THE GOOD GUYS are on the right, partially hidden in the trees in this artist's conception of the possemen's attack on the Confederate invaders. Photo—Denver Public Library.

TYPICAL GOLD SEEKER camp near Fairplay just before the Civil War and the downfall of town tough guy, Jim Reynolds. Photo—Colorado Historical Society.

THE DREDGE scarred valley of the Platte at Fairplay, where the Reynolds brothers joined the first abortive attempt to bring Colorado under the Stars and Bars.

ROBBING A BUCKSKIN COACH.

"THROW DOWN THE BOX" could be the caption for this classic interpretation of Jim Reynolds and his helpers looting the Buckskin stage. Photo—Denver Public Library.

JIM REYNOLDS and his men, with one exception, were executed by their guards when barely out of sight of Denver. Photo—Denver Public Library.

Denver Public Library

 *General Tarsney's War*

The two flat cars being hauled slowly up the mountainside from Cripple Creek to Victor on that bright May morning in 1894 were loaded with men who had a reputation for being tough. They were well armed and laughing and joking as they headed for what they were sure would be a short, and for them, safe battle with a bunch of "red necked miners."

The men were members of the so-called deputy army that had been raised by the Cripple Creek mine owners to put down what had become a long and costly strike. Most of the men had been recruited from the streets of Denver, most of them former police officers who had been dismissed from the force for such varied activities as robbery, extortion and assault. The balance were the dregs of the Soapy Smith gang.

As the tiny engine labored up the steep grade the rocky ridges seemed to shake with the sound of a violent explosion. Their faces, which only a moment before had mirrored self assurance now began to show the signs of panic. They were showered with bits and pieces of the Strong Mine headworks; the pulleys, cogs and gears along with assorted pieces of scrap iron. They stared in amazement as the huge steam boiler shot skyward and decided that they had had enough. Anyone who played with that much dyanmite was too tough even for a bunch of Denver thugs.

The engineer, fortunately, was no more heroic than his passengers. He shoved the engine into reverse, ran the throttle all the way to the corner and sent the abbreviated train careening back down the hill. The miners found this precipitous retreat hilarious and decided to help things along a little bit by loading a flat car with more explosives and turned it loose in hot pursuit of the fleeing engine. It missed the deputies, jumping the track on a short curve, and ended up killing a milk cow and a few goats.

The trouble had all started in late January when the mine owners attempted to put into effect a new work schedule for the men. The owners felt that the workers should put in ten hours a day rather than eight with no increase in pay, at that time a princely three dollars a day. The miners quite naturally felt that eight hours was quite enough for the three dollars, so they formed a union, affiliated themselves with the Western Miners Federation and started to talk strike. The owners were above negotiating with a bunch of riff raff and promptly put the ten hour day into effect. Five hundred miners quit the shafts and went home.

John Calderwood, founding father of the Western Federation happened to be on a tour of Colorado at the time and lent not only his moral but financial support to the strikers. An outstanding leader in the early days of organized labor, he set about to prove to the owners, whose only previous contact with unions had been with the highly ineffective Knights of Labor, that they had a fight on their hands when they bucked either Calderwood or people he represented.

Calderwood's first concern was for the striker's creature comforts. He set up a kitchen, assessing those still at work fifteen dollars a month to support the project. And since poor men eat about the same amount of food and wear the same amount of clothing as the rich, he put the arm on area merchants for both food and cash. He then went to the small camp of Altman and settled down for a long battle.

Colorado's political climate couldn't have been better for Calderwood and the strikers. A populist governor, Davis H. Waite had just begun his administration. A man who opposed capitalism in whatever form it might be found he threw the weight of his office behind the striking Cripple Creekers. Waite bore the nick name "Bloody Bridles," the result of an inflammatory speech he had made, allowing that he would rather see blood run in the streets up to the horse's bridle rather than have one working man exploited by the rich and powerful.

Waite's appointees were of a like political persuasion. He named, as state Adjutant General, an obscure and cantankerous lawyer from Durango, Thomas J. Tarsney. Tarsney was a man almost totally devoid of friends, a situation caused by what might charitably be called an unfortunate personality. Conversely, Tarsney liked almost no one, including the governor whom he persisted in referring to as "that damned old fool." But his dislike was even more intense for millionaires, so he could be counted on to carry out the orders of the governor.

The mine owners were hard to convince that they had a real strike on their hands. They felt that like the strikes at Leadville and Creede, this one would be over as soon as the miners were hungry enough. But these men had the advantage of having a genuine leader. Calderwood, recognizing his limitations, felt that he should appoint someone to take charge of the armed confrontation he was sure would come. He finally named two assistants to lead the fighting: Junius Johnson, a West Point drop out (or kick out) and Jack Smith who had recently been released from the prison at Canyon City.

Johnson had run afoul of the powers at West Point his senior year for overly enthusiastic hazing of under classmen and allowed to resign. He had come west to avoid bumping into former classmates. Smith's greatest virtue, from Calderwood's viewpoint, was his control of a group of highly organized and extremely competent toughs who could be counted on to back the miners when things got tough. These men, former classmates of Smith's at the pen, were currently engaged in the dangerous business of highgrading.

The first serious confrontation came about in March, 1894, causing El Paso County Sheriff Frank Bowers to have second thoughts about sheriffing as a way of life. Being a politician he hated to upset anyone who could find their way to the polls on election day. But when the owners obtained an injunction to prevent the strikers from interfering with the operation of the mines, it was up to Frank to deliver it. With both sides approaching the boiling point, Bowers was in a very uncomfortable position.

No matter the consequences, the court informed Bowers, he must serve the injunction. Bowers would have much preferred to continue his daily rounds of the saloons and the red light district, but orders were orders so he set out, rather grimly, to do his duty.

When Frank hesitantly rode into Altman the miners, who had been expecting the worst, felt that now the worst was here in the shape of the sheriff. They surrounded Bowers muttering threats against both the sheriff and the judge. Bowers, throat dry as sandpaper, read off the names of those who were required by the court to behave and hurried back to Cripple to have a little drink to calm his nerves.

The Sheriff had barely placed foot on rail when he got some more bad news. The miners, according to the report, had surrounded the Victor Mine and were threatening to destroy it. Bowers, with the press of business in town, felt that he couldn't be spared to make another trip up the mountain so he promptly deputized six or eight men, loaded them in a wagon and told them to get up there and protect that mine.

The deputies were gone what seemed an unreasonable length of time when the sheriff, worrying about his helpers, canvassed the saloons and called the rest of the unemployed citizens to arms. Just as Bowers started out on what he was sure was his date with martyrdom, the missing lawmen returned. Bowers felt that this called for a celebration so they all adjourned to a handy bar with both old and new deputies taking part in the county financed party.

The deputies sent to the Victor reported that they had not been mistreated but they had been told to get off Bull Hill and stay off. Bowers felt that such an order to representatives of the law was more than he could handle so he wired the governor, requesting that militia be sent. The problem was compounded when, during the night, the owners had leaflets distributed announcing that the mines would reopen the next day under armed guard. Since most of those available for deputy work were still feeling the effects of the night before, Bowers sent still another telegram pleading for help.

Calderwood, meanwhile, armed the miners on what was starting to be known as the Kingdom of Bull Hill. He posted pickets and issued passes, without which no one could pass the picket line. Then he and his "generals," Johnson and Smith, sat back to await the invasion that they were sure was coming.

On receipt of the telegrams from Bowers, Waite didn't exactly send the militia. Instead he did the next worst thing, sending his not too diplomatic adjutant general to the scene with a small escort. Tarsney conferred with the sheriff but about the only information he got from Bowers was that Bull Hill was under the control of a bunch of bushy haired, wild eyed anarchists and the only salvation was armed intervention by state troops.

Tarsney asked if the so called anarchists had put up any armed resistance to regularly appointed officers in the discharge of their duties. Bowers replied that they hadn't exactly done that, but they were talking tougher by the day. He was informed that only when the shooting started and presumably after someone had been killed would the militia intervene. Bowers, to prove his point, promptly set out for Colorado Springs to get some warrants so that the miners would have something to resist. Tarsney agreed to stay on the scene and see what luck the sheriff had serving the warrants before returning to Denver.

No sooner had the sheriff left the Palace Hotel than Tarsney sent word to Calderwood. Meeting the leader in his room, Tarsney warned Calderwood that warrants were on the way and that if the miners resisted service, Tarsney would have to use the militia to serve them. He added that once the militia was on the scene the owners could recruit labor and reopen the mines, winning the strike.

Calderwood assured Tarsney that the state had no worries so far as the conduct of the miners was concerned. The strikers had no wish to embarrass the administration and no member of the Federation would resist service. But, Calderwood continued, if you have militia anywhere in town, please keep them out of sight lest the strikers get nervous and commit some overt act.

Bowers returned with the warrants to find that even the escort had disappeared and only the general himself was on hand to lend what moral support he could. Bowers was stunned. He told Tarsney that he hadn't hired out to be a hero or a corpse and that he had been assured by the strikers that if he set foot on Bull Hill they would make his wife a widow.

Tarsney made some sympathetic noises and assured the sheriff that all would be well on the hill. All Bowers had to do was take the warrants up to Altman, serve them and bring his prisoners back to Cripple. All this talk, according to Tarsney, about violence was pure balderdash.

The sheriff remained unconvinced but since he already had the warrants in hand there was no way out. He wrote a farewell note to his friends and constituents, buckled on his gun, straightened his hat and went on his way. Expecting to be cut down any minute, he rode into Altman looking over his shoulder.

He couldn't have been more surprised by his reception in the Kingdom. He was met by Calderwood and the seventeen men named in his warrants and taken to the best saloon in town. After he had been treated to a drink all of the men told him how happy they would be to accompany the sheriff back to Cripple Creek and face whatever charges there were against them. Whether Bowers was the hero of the hour or not, he felt it when he returned from his journey into the forbidden land of the strikers with his prisoners.

Bowers soon found that he had been had by Tarsney. As soon as he and his prisoners passed the picket line, armed guards once again took up their positions on the slopes and once again entry was by Calderwood pass only. The prisoners were promptly arraigned and tried for their crimes. They were just as promptly acquitted. Their lawyer, by some strange coincidence, was that defender of the constitution, Thomas J. Tarsney, the man who had been called from the capitol to put down lawlessness in El Paso County.

The strike got out of hand with the departure of Calderwood in April of '94 to make a swing through other Colorado mining camps. Leaving "Generals" Johnson and Smith in command of the strike was much like leaving the fox in charge of the hen house. Johnson was a little short on scruples while Smith was totally devoid of morals. Smith, being the leader of the local hoodlum set, took charge and things immediately began to deteriorate.

The Smith boys heaped their first indignities on the heads of two men suspected of being spies for the owners. The two were caught at a miner's meeting and carted to Altman where they were forced to drink from a cuspidor prior to being run out of camp. Some of the more fun loving boys dropped one of the men down an abandoned shaft, breaking his leg, as the two spies were being escorted from Bull Hill.

As soon as the two hobbled, (gagging, one would imagine) back to Cripple, the owners who were, in the final analysis no better than the strikers, held their two bully boys up as paragons of all the good old American virtues and loudly proclaimed that revenge would be swift and just.

Johnson, upon hearing that the owners planned to set their dogs on the miners, promptly went to work. He constructed a fort of sorts on a cliff overlooking Altman complete with a log painted to look like a cannon. Being a West Pointer and well versed in modern weaponry, he also contrived a catapult to hurl dynamite bombs on the heads of any invaders. He then laid out a mine field on the approaches to the town and settled back to await developments.

The longer the owners delayed the attack the more bored the members of the Smith gang became. When they ran out of sheriffs or spies to mistreat, they would casually take a saloon apart, rob a store or take over one of the parlor houses. This type of activity got full coverage in the local press. The ordinary people, those who had to go to work every morning to keep groceries on the table, were already pretty well fed up with both the strike and some of the strikers and felt strongly that those who broke the law should be caught and punished. They were sick of living in a reign of terror.

Much of the uproar occurred in Colorado Springs where the residents were quite loud in their denunciation of the "anarchists." Talk, however, was one thing; taking a chance on being hit with a charge of dynamite was something else again. The Springs folks had an out; they had a lot more money than they had blood, so why not hire someone to keep the strikers in their place, which was on the other side of the Front Range. So saying they set out to recruit the motley crew that was put to flight by flying machinery and the flat car loaded with explosives.

After the first batch of deputies were put to flight the strikers engaged in an orgy of destruction. The miners cared no more for the rich folks in Little London, as they called the Springs, than the Londoners had for them. Smith and his group of thugs boiled over, looting stores and firing buildings.

Loading his drunken followers on wagons filled with dynamite Smith set out with the avowed intention of blowing every mine head, every office, every owner's house in the district. They had the poor judgment, however, to start on a mine owned by the one man who had supported the strike from the beginning, Winfield Scott Stratton.

Stratton, a former carpenter and Cripple's richest gold king, had not only recognized the union but had risked the hatred of his fellow owners by signing a contract with them. He changed sides when he heard that the strikers had taken over his fabulously rich Independence. He joined the other Springs millionaires in keeping the wires hot both to Washington and President Cleveland and Denver and Governor Waite. Between telegrams they passed the time circulating a petition calling for Waite's impeachment. They even started forming a Home Defense Force whose avowed purpose was to "wrest Bull Hill from the hands of the insurgents." There were also the usual pronouncements about defending the fair womanhood of the Springs and perhaps hanging General Tarsney just for the hell of it.

Gunmen were hired from as far away as Leadville with Stratton, still mad about the loss of his mine, offering to hire and equip an entire battalion to regain his property. Sheriff Bowers had hardly a moment to himself as he swore in something like a thousand volunteer deputies from among both the hired guns and the young fire eaters recruited in the Springs. Finally they were all gathered together and hauled across Hayden Divide where they encamped and established a headquarters.

Just when the owners were all set to unleash their forces of justice on the miners, who should appear but that old enemy of capitalism himself, Bloody Bridles. He had heard that the trouble was getting out of hand and had come, uninvited, to try and get things straightened out. Especially since both of the belligerent parties had started acting as though this really was a war, even going so far as to establish truce zones where prisoners could be exchanged.

Waite, in all justice, did his best. He went to Altman where he asked for and received full power to negotiate on the union's behalf with the owners. The miners assured the governor, though, that no matter the outcome of the talks on wages and hours, they would not give up until granted immunity from prosecution for any criminal acts with which they might be charged. Waite felt that this was reasonable, but found the owners had different ideas.

For five hours Waite and the owners beat on the table and shouted at one another. The owners agreed to the eight hour, three dollar day, but they planned to see that all of the miners who had participated in so much as a misdemeanor like spitting on the sidewalk were punished for their foul deeds. Both Waite and Calderwood, who had accompanied the governor to the meeting noticed as time passed, that a large crowed was gathered in front of the hotel, all talking rather loudly about ropes and trees.

A local judge made a speech to the crowd, holding them more or less spellbound while the governor and the union leader slipped out the back way and headed for the station. Only one man was on hand to bid them farewell, the beleaguered Sheriff Bowers. He handed the governor yet another request for the militia. The army of deputies gathered by the owners and recruited from the Springs had given the sheriff to understand that they were not under his orders. Bowers tried to impress on the governor that the time had come to get this whole mess settled and get all those gun toters, both amateur and professional, out of town and off the mountain.

The man that had emerged from the ranks and usurped the sheriff's power was a former shoe clerk and currently a county commissioner, one Boynton. Boynton felt that heaven had called him for this great mission and, being a politician, made no bones about his ability to lead the forces of right to a glorious victory. He made endless speeches, drilled the men to the best of his limited ability and plotted grand strategy for the assault on Bull Hill. It goes without staying that a victory would do much to advance his political ambitions.

Tarsney entrained the militia at Denver June 6th. When Boynton heard the news he immediately set his forces in motion. Bowers was appalled at the thought. He pleaded with them to give the strikers just a little more time, but to no avail. The army moved out, making camp two miles north of Altman that afternoon. Bull Hill appeared deserted so Boynton ordered an attack to drive the miners off in full retreat.

Up the hill went the amateur army, making good progress until they noticed that the air was filled with little popping noises. When pieces of rock began to shower them they realized that the miners were not only not retreating, but actually shooting at them. Pulling back that part of his army that hadn't already left at the first sound of hostile fire, Boynton decided to wait and mount a night attack. It failed as miserably as the daylight one had.

By the morning of the seventh the deputy army was considerably reduced. Many had strayed back down to Cripple and Victor to ward off the chill of the night with a nip or two. But it didn't matter. During the night the militia had arrived and taken up positions in a gully separating the defenders from the attackers. Tarsney approached Boynton and demanded that the deputies go home. Boynton, the bit in his teeth, refused. He tried a flanking attack but every time he got into position there stood the militia boys, right between those strikers and those set upon defending the ladies of Colorado Springs. Those same ladies were waiting breathlessly at home for word of a glorious victory over the forces of unionism and the Pope. As everyone waited, Tarsney sent units into Altman where the miners greeted them warmly. They, too were tired of playing soldier.

Tarsney executed a peace treaty between the parties June 10th, with the militia to stay on the job to make sure both parties behaved. The owners accepted the three dollar, eight hour day and Calderwood, along with nearly three hundred, of his followers were docketed for trial.

When the treaty was signed the volunteers headed for home, to be hailed as heroes and saviors of civilization as it was practiced in Colorado Springs. They held a parade up Tejon Street to the Courthouse where they were treated to speeches and cheers. At every mention of Waite and Tarsney, the crowd groaned loudly.

At the trial for the three hundred, only two were convicted, they being the men responsible for blowing up the Strong Mine. Calderwood, Johnson and Smith were speedily acquitted. Johnson later lost his life in the Spanish American War while Smith met his somewhat predictable end in an Altman gun fight.

Tarsney came to the Springs, put on his other hat and served as defense counsel for the same men he had arrested as adjutant general. His motives, as usual, were suspect. It was hinted that he wanted to get even with the folks in the Springs more strongly than he wanted justice for his clients.

Being Tarsney he had trouble keeping his mouth shut even in the enemy's camp. Each evening he would hold forth in his hotel on his ability as a general and detail how he had outsmarted those smart alecks from the Springs. A little of Tarsney went a long way, even in Durango, let alone in the Springs. Some of the toughs hired for the war were still in Colorado Springs, ready to do anything for a buck. They were hired to kidnap Tarsney, which they did, taking him to the railroad yards where they gave him a thorough coating of tar and feathers, dumping him some distance from town.

Making his way to a ranch, Tarsney got some of the tar removed and contacted Denver. The governor sent a special train and a gallon can of benzine to pick him up, clean him off and get him home. Tarsney tracked down his kidnappers but they were brought to trial in Colorado Springs and quite readily acquitted. The General lost all the way around, being cited during the trial for contempt.

When the General came back to answer the contempt charge he came in full dress uniform and with a militia bodyguard to protect him, as he said, from the barbarians of Little London. He was convicted and fined forty dollars.

The strike was finally over but many years were to pass before the barrier of mutual suspicion was removed from the residents of the Springs and the miners of Cripple Creek. The miners couldn't forget the deputy army and the good Republicans on the flatlands couldn't forget Tarsney and Waite, helping remove both of them from office at the next election. The fort on the cliff crumbled under the weight of time and finally the last vestiges of the Kingdom of Bull Hill were erased from the mountains surrounding the golden bowl.

CRIPPLE CREEK *during its' boom days as the fifth largest gold producer the world has known. Photo—Colorado Historical Society.*

BENNETT AVENUE, *Cripple Creek, before the street car line was installed. Photo—Denver Public Library.*

PART OF THE *deputy army raised to put down the Cripple Creek strike.* —Denver Public Library.

ALTMAN, near the eleven thousand foot mark was headquarters for strikers. Photo—Denver Public Library.

ABOUT ALL THAT is left of Victor, a one time city between Cripple and Altman are the crumbling remains of what once were fine business buildings.

CRIPPLE (Myers Avenue shown here) is slowly succumbing to the ravages of time and neglect. New subdivisions are sprouting in the mountains nearby and partially reviving town.

THE VICTOR MINE when in full production. Photo—Denver Public Library.

HILLSIDE NEAR Victor covered with mine tailings and the remains of someone's one time bonanza.

JOHN CALDERWOOD, head of the Western Miners Federation who took charge of the Cripple strike. Photo—Denver Public Library.

GENERAL THOMAS J. Tarsney, Durango Lawyer who served as Adjutant General in the Waite administration who wound up wearing a coat made of tar and feathers.

GOVERNOR DAVIS H. "Bloody Bridles" Waite, Populist leader of Colorado during the strike. Photo—Denver Public Library.

TINY NARROW gauge engines once hauled ore from the mines to the mills as well as hauling deputies back and forth up and down the hill. These are once again in service hauling tourists a short distance into the mountains after having been rescued from the jungles of Central America.

GULCH OUTSIDE of Cripple Creek near location of original strike made by cowboy Bob Womack.

BENNETT AVENUE in Cripple Creek. Most of striker-owner meetings were held in Palace Hotel. Photo—Denver Public Library.

 *The Court That Never Adjourned*

If the hanging on the courthouse steps in Fairplay the morning of April 28, 1880 hadn't shaken Judge Thomas M. Bowen enough, then the carefully coiled rope, complete with hangman's knot that had been left on his desk that same morning certainly caused that gentleman to have second thoughts about continuing the current term of court in Park County, Colorado. The judge, showing considerable wisdom, left town immediately and as a result the spring, 1880, term of court has not, to this day, been adjourned.

Judge Bowen had been involved the day before in two murder trials and had rendered his verdict in each of them. One, the State versus Cicero Simms, charged with the murder in January of 1880 of one John Johnson in the nearby town of Alma had been disposed of in a manner that apparently met with public approval. Simms was to be hanged. But the other, that of John J. Hoover, a Fairplay resident and operator of a local billiard parlor and saloon had met with vocal disapproval and ended with a lynching in the early morning hours. Simms, whose life was spared for a legal hanging, came out better in the long run than his jail mate, Hoover, who had gotten the best end when sentence was passed but whose life was ended at the hands "of masked men to the jury unknown" as the coroner's report put it.

Hoover was a long time resident of Colorado, having come to the goldfields in 1860, trying his luck first in the California Gulch diggings. He had moved across to mountains during the excitement at Buckskin Joe the following year and finally ended up at Fairplay when the mines were booming at Mount Bross and Lincoln. After settling in Fairplay he had entered the retail liquor and pool hall business, opening an establishment known as the Cabinet across from the Fairplay House. He lived in rather modest quarters attached to the Cabinet.

As a citizen Hoover left much to be desired. The general sentiment, expressed around town and in the columns of the local newspaper indicated that Hoover was barely tolerable, sober and a virtual terror when in his cups. That might have been acceptable but he spent most of his time sampling his own merchandise. He was, according to the Fairplay Flume, "charitably considered, when drinking, quite mad."

Throughout the spring of 1879 Hoover had been having trouble with the management of his neighbor, the Fairplay House. Water was distributed by ditch throughout the town and when the spring thaws came the Fairplay House ditch tended to overflow due to debris that had blocked the passage of the water. The water would overflow and run into Hoover's house and pool hall. Hoover, in his most diplomatic manner suggested to manager J.H. McClain that something be done about it, adding that it had better be damn quick.

McClain was aware of Hoover's violent disposition so he contacted one of his roomers, a currently unemployed former driver for the Wall and Witter Stage Line, Thomas H. Bennett, about putting in a day cleaning out the ditch to get Hoover off his back. Needing the money and seeing nothing dangerous about cleaning a ditch Bennett agreed to do the job, starting about mid morning, April 1, 1879.

Bennett took a shovel and set out to block the ditch a little upstream from the hotel. The blocking of the ditch proved to be a fatal error. No sooner had Bennett started to clean the blockage than the water ran over the temporary dam and straight into the home and business of Hoover. When Bennett saw what was happening he dug up the dam and hurried to Hoover's house where he apologized profusely to the lady of the house and assured her that it had not been his intent to cause her further problems with running water in the living room. He then returned to the hotel to check with McClain about where the ditch could be blocked to cause the least trouble.

When Bennett got to the hotel he found that McClain was taking a nap and his second in command, the desk clerk, was out of pocket. He waited for better than an hour, leaning on the desk and visiting with the three men who were in the lobby. While Bennett waited, Hoover emptied a bottle and dwelt upon the many mean things that the Fairplay house had visited on him. Along about two in the afternoon, filled to the brim with the fruit of the corn, he decided to take matters into his own hands and see that he was no longer put upon. Getting his pistol from under the bar he staggered casually over to the hotel.

As Hoover entered the lobby he saw Bennett leaning on the desk, apparently undisturbed by the water in Hoover properties. Although Bennett was obviously unarmed, Hoover drew his gun, pointed it at Bennett and proclaimed,

"I own that house and lot and I'm not going to have my family imposed on or you talking to my wife . . ."

Bennett was understandably frightened, throwing up his arms to protect himself from the pistol whipping he was sure Hoover planned for him, and answered,

"Hold on now. I don't want any trouble and I sure don't want to impose on anyone."

He had barely gotten the words out of his mouth when Hoover fired, the ball passing through his chest, out his back and falling on the floor. Bennett slumped over the desk, trying to hold himself erect, Hoover raising the pistol again shouting,

"Get up there, God Damn you . . ."

Just as Hoover was about to pull the trigger again, the girls who worked in the dining room came into the lobby to see what the fuss was all about. Hoover turned his gun on the girls and said,

"Get back in there where you belong. This is none of your business."

The girls, faced by a madman with a gun, promptly complied as Hoover turned once again to Bennett, only to have his arm caught by one of the bystanders who begged him not to shoot again.

The words finally penetrated Hoover's alcoholic haze. He pocketed the revolver and staggered from the hotel, headed more or less for the business district. His wife, having heard the shots from the hotel and knowing the mood of her husband when he was well filled, ran to the lobby, expecting to find the dead body of her husband but instead saw Bennett's corpse on the floor in a pool of blood. She then ran from the hotel in hopes that she could find John before he could do any more damage with the five rounds left in his gun.

Mrs. Hoover caught up with her gun wielding spouse and persuaded him to return to the Cabinet with her to await the coming of Sheriff Ifinger. By the time the sheriff had arrived, Mrs. Hoover had her husband more or less calm and ready to surrender to the law.

As soon as Hoover was jailed, the crowd began to gather on the courthouse lawn. Although Bennett had left his native Iowa barely a year before to come to the mining camps, he was apparently well thought of. Besides, most of the residents of Fairplay felt that Hoover had committed a totally senseless crime, killing a man he knew only by sight if at all. Sheriff Ifinger, sure that tempers would flare even higher after the town loafers had had a few, promptly made arrangements to transfer his prisoner to the Denver jail where he would be safe from mob violence until he could be brought to trial.

The trial was slightly over a year in coming. Apparently it wasn't too easy to decide who was to dispense justice in the Colorado hinterlands, since Fairplay was without judges for the year following the crime. Judge Bowen finally got the nod from the state legislature after more than ninety ballots had been cast to determine who got to be judge this year. In April, 1880 the judge finally came to Fairplay to hold court, trying, among other cases, that of John J. Hoover.

When Hoover returned to the scene of the crime, the Flume noted that about the only changes a year in jail had made in Hoover was the loss of the ruddy skin tone that had been so apparent when Hoover lived where a good (or even bad) drink could be had from time to time. The reporter also noted that Hoover seemed not the least upset by his upcoming trial, feeling sure that the past year had tempered some of the bad feeling so evident immediately after the shooting.

The trial was brief, the deliberations of the jury were even shorter. Testimony was given by the men who had been present in the lobby that fateful day; the girls in the dining room whom Hoover had threatened and finally the findings of the Coroner's Jury that clearly stated "Thomas Bennett met his death as a result of a bullet fired by John J. Hoover on April 1, 1879."

With the guilty verdict in hand, Judge Bowen called on Hoover to stand and face the bench so that sentence could be passed. Being both a judge and a politician the judge naturally couldn't resist this opportunity to make a speech, relating the history of the case and dwelling at some length on the year that Hoover had already spent in jail. Finally, the judge said, this man doesn't seem a danger to the community, so he will be sentenced to eight years at Canyon City.

The crowd was dumbfounded. Hoover flashed a big smile and turned to the crowed and said,

"That's fine. I'm a friend of H.A.W. Tabor (the Leadville Silver King and a power in Colorado Republican politics) and he'll see that I'm out in a year."

The words were ill chosen and spoken at just the wrong time. The crowd surged toward the rail, shouting threats against the life of both Hoover and the Judge, the judge pounding his gavel and call sheriff calling for order. When the room was finally cleared, Sheriff Ifinger took his charge up to the cell and the trial of Cecero Simms ordered to begin.

Every bar in town did a booming business that afternoon with those who felt that justice had fallen on her blindfolded face. No one, it was argued, in their right mind could fail to see that Hoover was the one man in all the county who really deserved to be hung. Any man who would shoot another over something as simple as an overflowing ditch really should be hung, or shot, or something. Then as the sun began to set, notices were posted around town warning those that wished to avoid trouble to be off the streets before midnight. Some of the talkers were apparently about to become actors.

Sheriff Ifinger noted the posters and stayed on extra late at the jail with the two guards he had hired to protect Hoover from violence. Finally, along about half past two the town seemed quiet with little or no traffic on the streets. The sheriff decided to call it a day and walked to his nearby house. Just as he relaxed in bed there was a loud knocking on the door.

The sheriff asked the callers what they wanted and further asked if whatever their business was, couldn't it wait until the next day. He was assured that the business had to be handled promptly and told the sheriff to open the door immediately. The sheriff refused so the men started to batter the door down. Mrs. Ifinger, now thoroughly frightened, opened the door and was faced by a group of armed, masked men variously estimated at from ten to twenty. As they crowded into the room they demanded that the sheriff give them the keys to the courthouse and the jail. Once again the sheriff refused, saying that even if he had the keys he wouldn't give them to a mob.

The men then told the sheriff to get dressed and go with them to the jail, assuring him that no harm would come to either the sheriff or his family if he obeyed orders. The sheriff hastily dressed and accompanied the men toward the jail, followed by Mrs. Ifinger barefooted and in her nightdress. As they passed the Fairplay House, Mrs. Ifinger entered the lobby to raise an alarm, but her calls were greeted with total silence. Even then most people didn't really want to be involved.

The masked men left the sheriff under guard near the courthouse while six of them proceeded to the building and another was sent back to the sheriff's house to hunt for the keys. Apparently they were not too familiar with the job of breaking into jails since no one ever thought to search the sheriff who had the keys in his pocket. Finding the door to the courthouse padlocked they set to work with heavy hammers and soon gained entrance.

Once inside the building, they headed for the jail, knocking on the door to the guardroom and demanding entrance. Taylor advised that no one could enter without permission from the sheriff. Continued pounding finally brought Taylor to the door where he was met by armed men who obviously meant what they were saying. Beach and Taylor were disarmed and led from the courthouse and asked for the keys to the main door of the jail as well as the keys to the cells. The men were told that no one had any keys, so back they went to the courthouse where they proceeded to batter down the main door. They then removed the door of Hoover's cell.

According to Simms, Hoover was quite unstrung by this turn of events, especially since he had been so pleased earlier with the sentence passed by the court. As the protesting Hoover was dragged from the cell he pleaded with the lynchers to spare him.

"Add ten years to my sentence," he begged, "give me a chance, anything but this."

His pleas were cut short when one of the masked men replied, "We'll give you the same chance you gave Bennett. None."

As they reached the entrance to the courthouse, his entreaties became more personal. He begged his captors to let him at least write a letter to his family. Simms started to interrupt the proceedings but decided to let well enough alone when one of the men turned to him and said,

"We don't have time for you tonight. We'll come back and get you tomorrow."

The midnight avengers, as the Flume called them, took Hoover to the steps of the courthouse and a rope was passed down from a second story window. The knot was tied and Hoover raised, kicking and strangling, into the air. The rope was made fast inside the building and the lynchers went on their way.

By the time Ifinger, Taylor and Beach reached Hoover it was too late, life was gone. Taylor and Beach recovered their weapons from the steps where the lynchers had left them and fired four shots to raise an alarm, but the men who had dealt their own kind of justice had disappeared among the dark streets of Fairplay.

Judge Bowen had been apprised of the lynching before he came to his office, but he wasn't prepared for what he found once he arrived for work. There, on his desk in addition to the noose, was a crudely drawn skull and crossbones and a brief note that indicated that the town hadn't been known for the past twenty years as Fairplay for nothing. The judge promptly packed and left, never to return. Even in later years, when he was campaigning for Senator, Bowen gave Park County a wide berth.

One of the old timers, quoted in a Denver paper nearly fifty years later, said that the judge might have remembered the Carmody case that had occurred earlier in the year. It seems that Sam Porter had taken on more than his share of cheap whiskey and decided that it would be fun to shoot the first man he met on the street. The man happened to be John Carmody, who walked around the corner of the livery stable just as Porter had made this decision. Carmody fell with a bullet between the eyes.

Rather than wait for a trial, some of the folks decided to end Porter's life of crime before it went any further. They nailed a crossarm about ten feet from the ground on the jail wall and promptly dispatched the marksman.

The lynchers failed to return for Simms the next night, leaving his legal hanging to be reported in a small space between an ad for a Chinese laundry and a notice about some truly exotic new ladies wear offered by Lieberman and Berkson, owners of the Boston Bazar, Alma, Colorado.

Fairplay is now a quiet filling station and restaurant town at the junction of two highways. A huge abandoned dredge lies just south of town on the road to Hartzel in the bed of the South Platte, an indication that things were once better (or worse, if you count the hangings and shootings) in this elderly collection of buildings that once were romance but now is just another town.

MAIN STREET, Fairplay, 1972. Although near such booming ski resorts as Breckinridge, just over Hoosier pass to the north beyond snow capped peak, little of the new found tourist excitement has rubbed off on the town.

ABANDONED MINES, some of which still seem to be in operating condition, cover mountains above Fairplay, all well posted with no trespassing signs.

VIEW OF FAIRPLAY about time of Hoover lynching. Significance of two grave cemetery is not known. Photo—Denver Public Library.

PARK CITY, up Mosquito Gulch from Fairplay was once one of many booming camps in the Park County country. Some say it, rather than Fairplay was the scene of the Carmody killing and Porter lynching.

JUDGE AND LATER Senator Thomas Bowen never adjourned court in Fairplay during spring term of 1880. A coiled rope, complete with hangman's knot on his desk hastened his departure. Photo—Denver Public Library.

FAIRPLAY COURTHOUSE in 1880's. Roof over steps must have been built to make lynching from the second story a little more difficult. Photo—Denver Public Library.

FAIRPLAY in the early 1880's when rich gold and silver mines made it a metropolis of central Colorado. Photo—Denver Public Library.

MAIN STREET, Fairplay, about 1880. Photo—Denver Public Library.

Another Quality Publication By

Nortex Press